THE STRATEGIC PLAN THAT EMPOWERED
SAN DIEGO ZOO GLOBAL
TO LEAD THE FIGHT AGAINST EXTINCTION

the Call

THE STRATEGIC PLAN THAT EMPOWERED
SAN DIEGO ZOO GLOBAL
TO LEAD THE FIGHT AGAINST EXTINCTION

BETH BRANNING

SAN DIEGO ZOO GLOBAL **PRESS**

The Call: The Strategic Plan That Empowered San Diego Zoo Global to Lead the Fight against Extinction was published by San Diego Zoo Global Press in association with Beckon Books. Through these publishing efforts, we seek to inspire readers to care about wildlife, the natural world, and conservation.

San Diego Zoo Global is committed to leading the fight against extinction. It saves species worldwide by uniting its expertise in animal care and conservation science with its dedication to inspire a passion for nature.

Douglas G. Myers, President and Chief Executive Officer
Shawn Dixon, Chief Operating Officer
Yvonne Miles, Corporate Director of Retail
Georgeanne Irvine, Director of Corporate Publishing

San Diego Zoo Global
PO Box 120551
San Diego, CA 92112-0551
sandiegozoo.org | 619-231-1515

San Diego Zoo Global's publishing partner is Beckon Books, an imprint of Southwestern Publishing Group, Inc., 2451 Atrium Way, Nashville, TN 37214. Southwestern Publishing Group is a wholly owned subsidiary of Southwestern/Great American, Inc., Nashville, Tennessee.

Christopher G. Capen, President, Southwestern Publishing Group
Kristin Stephany, Director of Partner Development, Southwestern Publishing Group
Kristin Connelly, Managing Editor, Southwestern Publishing Group
Betsy Holt, Publisher, Beckon Books
Vicky Shea, Senior Art Director/Interior Design
Lori Sandstrom, Cover Design/Interior Graphics
swpublishinggroup.com | 800-358-0560

ISBN: 978-1-935442-72-1 (hardcover)
ISBN: 978-1-935442-73-8 (softcover)
Library of Congress Control Number: 2018953749

Printed in the United States of America
10 9 8 7 6 5 4 3 2 1

This book is dedicated to Douglas G. Myers.
Without his visionary leadership, The Call would
never have come to life.

CONTENTS

HEEDING THE CALL

Douglas G. Myers
President/CEO, San Diego Zoo Global

T he story of The Call strategic plan is about both honoring the past and embracing the future. It represents more than 100 years of progress for the San Diego Zoo and for the many people whose passion built this organization. Strong leaders among the staff and the board of trustees gave us a firm footing that allowed us to remain resilient through both the good years and the tough times. Now, the current plight of wildlife requires us to grow and evolve, and The Call is a blueprint for that evolution.

The Call is changing our organization into a business dedicated to leading the fight against extinction. Saving species is not a sprint—it's a marathon. We're in it for the long haul. We do not intend to save species on our own; in fact, The Call hinges on our ability to become better collaborators. Our goal is to bring partners together and serve as facilitators for many complex conservation efforts. Preventing species extinction is a puzzle with numerous pieces, but we are devoted to filling in the gaps.

Let me tell you the story of the ʻalalā (pronounced ah-luh-LA). This crow species has lived on the Hawaiian Islands since before humans settled there but has been extinct in the wild since 2002. These animals are big and black with a striking glossy sheen to their feathers. You might be thinking, "So what? They're just crows." Like all species, they play an important part in their ecosystem. In the case of the ʻalalā, that role is to spread seeds of native plants throughout the forest.

1

We started working with the ʻalalā in 1996, when just 20 birds remained. The Peregrine Fund had set up two bird conservation centers in Hawaii in 1993, in partnership with the US Fish and Wildlife Service and the Hawaiian government. These centers were transferred to San Diego Zoo Global (SDZG) in 2000. Having both the Keauhou and Maui centers ensured that the precious ʻalalā had an assurance population: if something happened to one facility, the species would be safely sheltered elsewhere.

Breeding ʻalalā in managed care has been difficult, as the birds have unique qualities that present challenges for raising their chicks. Each mating pair needs its own aviary, and infertile eggs are common. The ʻalalā are extremely choosy about their mates, and the males sometimes interfere with egg laying and incubation. They require around-the-clock care at both of our conservation centers. It has always been our goal to release the birds into the wild, so they are raised without seeing their human caretakers. Our keepers monitor them on video and even use ʻalalā hand puppets to feed chicks and administer medication.

By 2016, we had expanded the population of captive ʻalalā to 125 birds and were finally ready to release them into the wild. We spent months training them to fear their natural predators, such as the ʻio, a native hawk, and to navigate situations that would likely come up in the wild. The training culminated in the triumphant release of five birds in Keauhou, on the island of Hawaii. Days later, though, three birds were dead. Two had been attacked by the ʻio, while another bird starved to death. The two remaining birds were retrieved and relocated back into the conservation center.

As new chicks hatched, we stepped up our training to address the situations they would encounter in the wild. In 2017, we released 11 birds. In 2018, they were all present and accounted for. They even changed their vocalizations to a new kind of *caw* that keepers had never heard from the birds in managed care. Our scientists think this may be an adaptation that is helping them survive in their new forest home. However, in 2018, the ʻalalā faced another threat: this time from the Kilauea volcano eruption. Once again, we were forced to adjust, making contingency plans to evacuate the birds to safer quarters if needed.

This is how wildlife conservation stories unfold. It is rarely a straight line between helping an endangered species and then seeing them successfully reintroduced to the wild. It is often a bumpy road with many stops and starts. SDZG has taken on the role of fighting extinction, and we are committed to helping the ʻalalā.

Our unwavering commitment is to ensure that every animal in our care is given the opportunity to thrive and flourish. These animals are ambassadors for their wild counterparts, and they inspire people to care about wildlife in a way books, videos, and even virtual reality can't match. Protection and preservation have always been central to our guiding principles—and will be as long as we exist.

Many wonderful organizations help wildlife, and we are privileged to partner with dozens of them. As for our staff, volunteers, and board members, The Call strategic plan has made them particularly proud of the work they do on behalf of SDZG. These efforts have harnessed our passion, allowing us to spread our wings and work to lead the fight against extinction . . . one species at a time.

TALE OF TRANSFORMATION

"This plan is a call to action: to awaken the world to the plight of wildlife—and to provide hope for the future of nature."
The Call, the strategic plan of San Diego Zoo Global

The San Diego Zoo began as a menagerie more than a century ago, serving as a favorite destination for people who delighted in the company of animals. Visitors grew to love the beauty of our flora and the majesty of our fauna. Over the years, the Zoo expanded and adapted, becoming more innovative and eventually garnering a worldwide reputation as a premier family destination. The San Diego Zoo's parent organization, then called the Zoological Society of San Diego, thrived as a business as well, even adding a second wildlife facility under the leadership of an enthusiastic staff and a dedicated board of trustees.

By the mid-1970s, however, it became clear to us that wildlife populations around the world were in desperate trouble. As natural ecosystems surrendered to the growing demands of humanity, the planet was experiencing a species decline that was unprecedented within the last 65 million years of life. Without a rescue plan, we knew thousands of endangered animal and plant species would be lost in an unraveling of ecosystems that would impact all life on Earth.

In 1975, the San Diego Zoo created a scientific branch to study these complex conservation issues affecting endangered animals and plants. As the perils for wildlife intensified, our conservation scientists and animal-care specialists grew in number and passion, their scientific research efforts funded in part by the nonprofit revenues of the San Diego Zoo. Soon, we were helping animals on a grand scale and garnering respect from conservationists around the world.

A Critical Juncture

Around the turn of the 21st century, however, the San Diego Zoo came to a crossroad. With the economy in turmoil and traditional funding sources drying up, we struggled to sustain both our conservation, animal-care, and visitor-engagement efforts. Yet how could we choose to focus on one at the expense of the other? The San Diego Zoo and its sister facility, which later became known as the San Diego Zoo Safari Park, were beloved by families from around the world. Although our parks struggled with visitor decline during economic tough times, they brought in the revenue needed to keep the organization afloat. The Zoo and Safari Park also provided homes for thousands of animals, representing nearly 900 species and subspecies. Still, our organization—and, in fact, much of the world—could no longer justify sheltering zoo animals unless they were part of a larger conservation and education solution.

The Call outlines the story of how our parent company, which came to be known as San Diego Zoo Global (SDZG), made strategic choices to solve these problems, ultimately creating a solution that was beyond the imagination of anyone involved at the time. The solution required informed risk-taking, visionary thinking, and an unwavering commitment to robust strategic planning and strong management principles. Through many setbacks and strides forward, this strategic plan eventually crystallized into a vision for a desired future and provided a roadmap to achieve that vision.

While you may not be grappling with wildlife conservation issues, chances are you do struggle to balance your organization's aspirations with the realities of its resources. It's also likely that you dream of exponential change for yourself or for your organization, but you can't imagine how you will get your stakeholders to rally around your dream. This process will change the way you look at strategic planning. We're confident it can work for you as well as it did for us.

A WAKE-UP CALL

WHY CHANGE?

"It is not the strongest or the most intelligent who will survive but those who can best manage change."
Charles Darwin

If you go to Kenya on a photo safari, you'll see wildlife everywhere: perched in the trees, peeking from behind bushes, and drinking from a nearby water hole. As you bounce across the unpaved roads in a weather-beaten safari truck, you might find an enormous ostrich perform an elaborate dance to impress his mate. You could spot a pride of lions sharing the remains of a gazelle. You're likely to see hippos eyeing you suspiciously from the river's edge.

What you probably won't see, though, are rhinos.

Rhinos used to range throughout Africa and Asia, but they have been continuously poached for decades. Today, the few remaining rhinos are protected in sanctuaries, national parks, or managed care facilities. There are five species of rhinos (white, black, greater one-horned, Sumatran, and Javan), and they're all endangered. They are threatened by relentless poaching driven by highly organized international crime rings that profit from the demand for rhino horns, particularly in Asia. Concoctions made from rhino horns have been prescribed in traditional Asian medicine for two millennia. Until the late 1800s, the effect on the species was manageable. By the early 1900s, however, the increase in demand for rhino horns and extensive trophy hunting had decimated white rhino populations and fewer than 20 individuals remained.

While the southern white rhino subspecies has rebounded, the situation for its cousin, the northern white rhino, has grown even more catastrophic. In the 1960s, there were approximately 2,000 northern white rhinos remaining; in 2018, only two were living. In 1970, there were 65,000 black rhinos in Africa; in 2018, that number was down to 5,000. And although significant efforts have been made to safeguard southern white rhinos, at least three are still being poached each day. The demand for rhino horns has, amazingly, escalated as a status symbol in recent years.

For 30 years, San Diego Zoo Global cared for three of the world's last remaining northern white rhinos. Today, the two remaining females live in Kenya, surrounded by armed guards to provide around-the-clock protection from poachers.

In addition to rhinos, many other species of animals and plants are rapidly disappearing. Sadly, the only place to see some endangered species in the future will be in a managed care setting such as the San Diego Zoo or the San Diego Zoo Safari Park. These facilities not only care for critically endangered species, providing enrichment, proper diet, health care, and overall welfare, but they also forge connections between people and animals, enabling people who could never afford a trip to Africa or Asia to see rhinos, giant pandas, tigers, and other endangered species up close. Studies show that this bond leads to a lifelong affinity for animals and a greater likelihood of taking a role in supporting them.

The fate of rhinos and other endangered species is what drives the thousands of decisions we make every day at SDZG. It's also what led us to create The Call, a new breed of strategic plan that radically transformed our organization.

Why Change?

In 2012, SDZG was a successful organization. We were reaping the rewards of more than 95 years of experience and a decade of deliberate change. We were a $240 million organization, bringing in nearly 5 million guests per year to the Zoo and the Safari Park. In fact, we had half a million members in a county of 3 million people, approximately 3,000 employees, and a dedicated cadre of volunteers. Our animal care standards had evolved significantly, along with our processes and our leaders.

By all accounts, SDZG was doing well. But for us, these successes were not enough. We wanted animals to flourish both in managed care *and* in the wild. We wanted the animals and plants in our parks to serve as ambassadors for their wild counterparts instead of the last representatives of dying breeds. We knew we had to do more for the world's wildlife, but we weren't sure how. Slowly, we tiptoed out from the safety of our successful business model, looking for ways to thrive as an organization while also helping endangered plants and animals to survive.

The Call is the strategic plan that guided our transformation, enabling us to identify our unique contribution to the wildlife conservation landscape. Launching The Call in 2015 also helped us come to terms with how we could mesh our longstanding desire to aid animals and plants in the wild with our 100-year history of helping them thrive in managed care. The Call has provided thousands of employees and volunteers with an opportunity to see how they connect with this important work—whether they care for gorillas at the San Diego Zoo, sell soft drinks at the San Diego Zoo Safari Park, or study jaguars in the wilds of Peru.

This is the story of how we developed, launched, and lived The Call, setting out on a multidecade odyssey to ensure a future for plants and animals. If you're interested in wildlife conservation, you'll be heartened to read about the many organizations working tirelessly for the cause. But this book is not a zoo story or even a conservation story. It's a book about the *value of strategic planning and leadership* to rally your supporters and help you rise above your barriers to success, regardless of the business you are in. Getting transformational results for your organization is vital; doing so will allow you to deliver on your mission. While you may keep your organization chugging along by making incremental changes, you'll need exciting results to move the needle on the gauge of significant success.

Insight and Experiences

In addition to sharing the specifics of The Call, we'll detail the organizational culture that preceded it, providing insight—both through successful initiatives and difficult challenges—that helped SDZG eventually create award-winning strategic planning and leadership methods.

Since launching The Call, our CEO, Douglas ("Doug") Myers, has been committed to sharing our experiences with collaborators so that everyone can contribute more to endangered species and to the wildlife-conservation community. We have facilitated planning processes for organizations, associations, work groups, teams, committees, individuals, cities, and even the continent of Australia.

This book is meant to extend that sharing of best practices and inspirational tales to the social sectors at large, particularly nonprofit organizations and associations that rely on philanthropy or membership. Our hope is that you'll use this collection of stories, plans, and methods to transform your own organization—to realize your unique mission and bring your distinct vision to life.

A "Different Breed" of Strategic Plan

The Call was the result of a planning evolution at SDZG. What separated it from its predecessors and other strategic plans?

- **It represented a willingness to take a huge risk.** It was an informed risk, based on research, but a scary change in direction for an organization that had done just fine for nearly a century. It managed to rise above the easier alternative of employing comfortable, incremental change.

- **It was the right idea at the right time.** After many years, the groundwork had finally been laid. For a decade, we had worked under our previous strategic plan, The Lynx, to shore up the infrastructure needed to set out in a new direction.

- **It had multiple horizons.** The Call required a decade-long commitment to its vision and mission but segmented this work into three- to five-year priorities and annual tactics. This allowed us to remain on course but to be flexible enough to adapt to changes in our environment.

- **It attracted funders and followers.** The Call and its actions inspired grants and donations that have run the gamut from a few dollars to game-changing gifts. It brought in a new type of donor interested in stemming the tide of extinction for plants and animals.

- **We lived the plan.** SDZG leaders have continued to make resource-allocation decisions based on The Call. Perhaps even more important, we communicate how our decisions relate to the plan so board members, staff, and volunteers can connect the dots.

CHAPTER

2

EXAMINING OUR CIRCUMSTANCES

"The great enemy of truth is very often not the lie—deliberate, contrived, and dishonest—but the myth—persistent, persuasive, and unrealistic. Too often we hold fast to the clichés of our forebears. We subject all facts to a prefabricated set of interpretations. We enjoy the comfort of opinion without the discomfort of thought."
John F. Kennedy

The first step in our strategic planning cycle was to take a hard look in the mirror. In 2001, San Diego Zoo Global conducted a robust environmental scan—also called an "environmental assessment"—that yielded a candid look at the feasibility of various business models that we might adapt moving forward.

During the environmental scan, we thoroughly examined the factors that could affect our future, using facts and information (instead of opinions) as decision-making criteria. The scan included an external look at marketplace trends, legislation on the horizon, opportunities within our sector, and threats faced by the organization. It also looked inward, scrutinizing the viewpoints of staff, board members, volunteers, and beneficiaries.

Frankly, many of us wanted to skip the environmental assessment. We assumed we knew all of the inner workings of our organization because we spent so much time immersed in the environment. In many ways, this was true . . . but we did discover some blind spots. Not everyone in the strategic planning process had the same level of understanding, and none of us had a full-circle view. We also didn't have a deep understanding of how everyone viewed the organization, internally or externally.

At SDZG, we assessed our environment in a number of ways. First, we surveyed various stakeholder groups that had some "skin in the game," including staff, volunteers, board members, collaborators, and colleagues. We asked them what they thought we were doing well, what we could improve, and what opportunities they saw for us. We cast a wide net for this, even though it was initially painful to hear what some people had to say.

We also kept our eyes open: in addition to upcoming legislation, we researched all the trends that affected SDZG's work, both current trends and those on the horizon. We looked at economic trends, giving trends, risk management trends, conservation trends, visitor trends, and leadership trends. We invited experts to make presentations on various scan-related topics, and we hosted a forum to discuss the future of zoos.

We resisted the urge to avoid trends for which we could find little information. And we pushed ourselves to face the problems that seemingly had no solution—in particular, how SDZG could provide top-notch care for animals, educate the public, conserve wildlife, and remain financially sustainable while doing so. After all, we would not be able to achieve transformative results by pretending that problems didn't exist or by overlooking the trends looming on the horizon. Ignoring these issues would have guaranteed the creation of a lackluster or misguided plan.

We also gathered information about our current state. While many of us knew a lot about our corner of SDZG, none of us knew everything.

We gathered our business plans, marketing plans, development plans, facility plans, financial plans, and initiative lists. We helped each other get up to speed on the areas in which we had deep individual (but not necessarily shared) knowledge.

"The environmental scans were very informative, and they showed us the gaps that we needed to fill," recalled Dwight Scott, Zoo director. "While we were conducting the scans, we uncovered so much information that I couldn't see how it would all be relevant. But it was really valuable to see those various perspectives."

Once the information was collected, we analyzed it by conducting a SWOT analysis of the internal Strengths and Weaknesses of the organization as well as the external Opportunities and Threats. Then we synthesized the information into an executive summary to be reviewed by the planning team. The environmental scanning process took six months to complete.

Painful Lessons

After we assessed many factors and considered dozens of possible future directions, we had to face the results. They were a bit disheartening. While many of us wanted to become a major conservation nongovernmental organization (NGO), the environmental assessment showed that we were not in a position to pull this off.

In our 2001 environmental scan, we found that:

- **Externally, SDZG was not widely viewed as a conservation organization.** This was an eye-opener. We had scientists around the world studying the conservation problems of various species, but the world did not yet see SDZG primarily as a provider of conservation solutions. Surveys showed we had not effectively communicated our conservation mission to the public. The public—and potential funders—simply saw SDZG as a great place for animal care and family entertainment. It was hard to hear, but the world didn't see us as a force for change in wildlife conservation.

- **Internally, we disagreed about our direction.** Although all of us wanted a future for SDZG that included wildlife conservation, we did not all agree on how this should come about. Some employees and board members were eager for SDZG to evolve into a conservation organization. Others felt that we should research conservation issues but continue to focus on the business we knew best—providing education and fun for Zoo and Safari Park visitors. As Berit Durler, former board chair and trustee emeritus, recalled, "Our strategic planning research showed that we could move toward a conservation-funding model, but many felt that it could kill the goose that lays the golden egg, [meaning that] our organization would no longer be financially sustainable. We weren't ready for the change, but it was the start of something that kept percolating."

- **Conservation "competition" was stiff.** SDZG was not big enough to "compete" for major conservation funding. We were shocked by the size of the gap between our own fundraising efforts and the level needed to become a major conservation NGO like the World Wildlife Fund or The Nature Conservancy. Those organizations did not have the significant overhead that was required to provide top-notch animal care and capital improvements to two wildlife parks year-round. Obviously, SDZG did, so the price of entry into that market was out of range for us. Of course, we would never consider lowering our animal welfare standards or closing our doors to guests. We knew that attempting to compete directly with other conservation organizations for funding was not the best way forward— however, we didn't yet have clarity about our own conservation niche.

- **Public perception of animal welfare had shifted.** Animal welfare had long been a focus for SDZG, but our assessment helped us realize that the public's *perception* of how animals were thriving was as important as the *fact* that they were thriving. Although we prided ourselves on using scientific evaluation of the animals' needs to drive habitat design, we realized guests would judge the animals' welfare by their human perspective: what they thought an enriching environment should be and how much space they perceived an animal might need. (For instance, the Zoo's meerkat habitat might look barren to some people, but the dirt landscape is intentional: meerkats need to be able to dig!) So SDZG not only had to provide the best care that science could offer, but we also had to ensure that guests recognized it as such.

- **Funding had become a growing concern.** The economy was in trouble in the early 2000s, and zoos across the United States were seeing flat attendance numbers. Meanwhile, people—including those of us at SDZG—were becoming less content with the idea of zoos as simply places to showcase animals and educate the public about wildlife. We were worried about maintaining the resources to thrive, especially as post-9/11 donation funding shifted away from conservation concerns and toward religious causes and education needs. As funding became a larger concern, we struggled to choose a vision that would allow us to help wildlife well into the future.

- **Many foundational issues needed to be addressed.** In 2001, our organization had evolved in many ways, but in other areas we remained behind the times. At SDZG, we had a strong culture of caring for wildlife, but we sharply disagreed about how to evolve from a zoo that did conservation into a conservation organization that inspired others by providing wildlife experiences. We needed to put processes into place to shore up infrastructure and build capacity among staff and board members.

- **A phased-in vision needed to be implemented.** Our visioning process in 2001 and 2002 led us to the realization that we would have to become a conservation organization in phases. The first phase would be to step up our game, over time becoming leaders in connecting people to wildlife and conservation. In the past, we'd fallen short of this goal, which is one reason the public did not see us as a conservation organization. We had struggled to engage people with our conservation stories or to change their behavior toward the environment. We knew we would have to boost our internal organization to find the resources and focus needed to achieve this vision.

Fast Forward 10 Years

By examining our internal shortcomings and zeroing in on these factors, we steadily moved toward the goal of becoming a conservation organization within 12 years. To assess our progress, we conducted the same review in 2012. We found that we had overcome some significant hurdles, but new trends and concerns had surfaced. Some of the key points from the second SDZG environmental scan showed that we needed to:

- **Provide authentic experiences.** By growing up in constant contact with technology, younger generations had created new social norms for experiencing the world. We recognized that the Zoo, Safari Park, and our global conservation efforts had the opportunity to provide authentic experiences that would hold a different kind of value—genuine, immersive experiences with nature and wildlife. However, SDZG needed to offer enhancements to social media, citizen science, communication, and learning in order to engage future generations. The demand for special experiences had increased significantly over the past several years, and we would have to expose future visitors to even more new opportunities.

- **Showcase the vision.** The environmental scans showed that we needed to design new animal experiences at the San Diego Zoo and San Diego Zoo Safari Park to demonstrate how we were fulfilling our vision. Each new addition would highlight how plants and animals were thriving under expert care as well as being "protected" in the wild (and sometimes even reintroduced into their native habitat). Following these experiences at the Zoo or Safari Park, guests might be moved to support our conservation vision.

- **Engage learners.** By creating a more immersive environment, we would empower young minds seeking knowledge and active skills for understanding and working in the world. Their contributions and participation would help to secure a future in which wildlife could thrive.

- **Change perceptions.** The public's perception of zoos was still evolving, along with its expectations. We realized it would be important to listen carefully to our critics. We also needed to demonstrate SDZG's contributions through action and activation across multiple channels of responsibility—including learning, conservation, science, and social engagement—and by emphasizing that SDZG was focused on creating opportunities for animals to thrive.

- **Make emotional connections.** We introduced visitors to living animal ambassadors, such as cheetahs, macaws, and servals. These on-site experiences showcased conservation expertise while creating an emotional connection with the natural world. As stewards of animal welfare, we sought to provide the context for people to appreciate animals and plants, motivating guests to take personal responsibility for changing the fate of wildlife.

- **Come to terms with the state of endangered wildlife.** SDZG's key message had to be one of hope, an optimistic expectation that we would do everything necessary to protect key species from extinction. However, despite a decades-long commitment to conservation—both on our part and on the part of numerous other organizations—animal and plant species were continuing to vanish at record speeds. For instance:
  - Population sizes of vertebrate species had decreased worldwide by more than 50 percent since 1970.[1]
  - In the wild, 41 percent of amphibian species were listed as threatened or extinct. What's more, one in five plant species was threatened with extinction.[2]
  - In SDZG's own backyard, Southern California remained one of the world's biodiversity hotspots, with a high proportion of critically endangered species, including Stephens' kangaroo rats, arroyo toads, and California gnatcatchers.[3]

- The loss of species around the world wasn't just impacting wildlife, it was also causing disruption in pollination, natural pest control, nutrient cycling, water quality, and human health.[4]
- From an economic standpoint, the value of losing biodiverse ecosystems was estimated to be 10 to 100 times the cost of maintaining them.[5]

Timing Is Everything

Despite these challenges, we had experienced a lot of positive developments since our first assessment in 2002. Our second environmental scan showed us that the timing was right for us to become more conservation focused.

We had strong partners who would work with us to advocate for legislation to provide the strongest protection for species. We had been invited to join forces with the US Department of State, the US Fish and Wildlife Service law enforcement unit, and USAID. All were leading efforts to combat the wildlife trade, which had an estimated value of $19 billion annually.[6] We had also partnered with other groups to help protect the Endangered Species Act (ESA)—the cornerstone of species conservation in the United States. (This act was, and continues to be, under threat.[7]) And the Association of Zoos and Aquariums was preparing to launch a new initiative to save at least 100 species, in which SDZG would play a key role.

We realized, however, that there was insufficient space in zoos to hold— let alone breed—the number of endangered species that would benefit from managed care populations.[8] To address this issue, SDZG formed the Alliance for Sustainable Wildlife in partnership with the Audubon Zoo in 2013. The alliance would serve as a model for how zoos could collaborate to increase the resources available to support assurance populations for plants and animals, and for how zoos could work together to implement reintroduction programs for vulnerable species. With this alliance, SDZG would transfer animals from

San Diego to a breeding facility in Louisiana. This would bolster populations of threatened and endangered species—such as giraffes, okapis, and bongos—that need large populations to create sustainable breeding groups.

Finally, the timing was right to capitalize on SDZG's longtime scientific efforts. Many conservation NGOs were de-emphasizing science in favor of ecosystem services and human-use approaches. This meant that they would require science-based partners such as SDZG to effectively conserve plant and animal species and manage natural resources.[9] Meanwhile, technological advances in genomics were bringing new importance to the SDZG Frozen Zoo® and other bio-banking efforts.[10] SDZG had the opportunity to become the hub of a global genetic rescue effort.

In short, we learned a great deal from the two environmental scans we conducted, garnering information such as how we were perceived as an organization, the challenges we faced as a global community, and the steps we needed to take to implement change. Katie Cox, a SDZG human resources benefits specialist, was part of the second environmental scanning process. She explained, "Recognizing that we're an organization without much staff turnover, and we've been here for decades, the environmental scans were extremely helpful. We needed the outside perspective. It was valuable to hear the trends and how we're viewed by others. It helped us understand where we truly stood as an organization."

PLAYING THE LONG GAME

"Good business leaders create a vision, articulate the vision, passionately own the vision, and relentlessly drive it to completion."
Jack Welch, leadership author and business executive

The Call was not the first time we tried to develop a conservation-based strategic plan. It was just the first time we were successful. We had many of the right elements in place during earlier attempts, but we came to realize that we could not leap from point A to point C without many stops along the way.

Strategic planning had been part of the DNA of San Diego Zoo Global since the 1980s. Early efforts allowed us to glimpse the benefits of agreeing on shared goals and tracking progress toward those goals. Our previous plans included a relevant mission and measurable indicators to help the board and staff at SDZG maintain focus and improve the organization. But as we began to adopt our first vision in the early 2000s, we soon realized that there were difficult compromises and trade-offs we were not yet prepared to make.

The turn of the millennium was a pivotal time in SDZG's history. The executive staff had previously been focused on vital issues such as animal welfare, employee enhancement, government regulations, and guest services. However, in 2002, we were facing a perfect storm of tough financial times and burgeoning conservation issues. These challenges forced us to take a hard look at the external world. Meanwhile, the tension between conservation and the guest experience framed our internal dialogue. As these dynamics played out, the board's confidence in our CEO, Doug Myers, lagged, and our passionate staff became increasingly outspoken about the future of wildlife.

Doug realized that we needed a shared vision for the future to get everyone working toward a common goal. He reorganized the staff to create a group to focus on issues of Vision, Innovation, and Strategy (VIS). Then we engaged consultants to help with our first-ever visioning process and to get the VIS group up to speed. Through this visioning process, we examined the state of the organization, the opinions of key groups, and the gaps between what we wanted to achieve and what we were delivering.

Dr. Allison Alberts, chief conservation and research officer, has been a veteran of many of SDZG's strategic planning efforts. She noted that people often hesitate to reach for something revolutionary: "There's always fear that becoming more strategic will result in unintended harm or make someone's job obsolete. You have to get past this fear and realize that you can have a bold vision and transformational strategies, but you have to trust the process." Allison also added that it's important to take time to acknowledge staff members' discomfort with change. "You have to make concessions to progress. Once people see that it's working, then they relax and you can move forward at a faster pace."

For SDZG, this led to an entirely different type of strategic plan in the early 2000s. Named The Lynx, the plan was designed to help us become a world leader in connecting people to animals and conservation by forging critical new links. Since the plan was focused on wildlife, an image of the lynx—a beautiful, solitary cat—became our symbol of change and the visual identity of the plan.

SDZG 21ST-CENTURY STRATEGIC PLANNING
TIMELINE

2002 — FIRST VISION STATEMENT
After a thorough environmental assessment, SDZG identifies its first vision statement: to become a world leader in connecting people to wildlife and conservation.

2003 — LAUNCH OF THE LYNX
The organization creates a strategic plan to achieve its new vision and dubs it The Lynx. It focuses on critical areas needed to bring the vision to life.

2006 — THE LYNX YEARS: A TRILOGY
A second Lynx plan begins in 2006. In all, there will be three Lynx plans implemented over the course of a decade, each plan bringing SDZG closer to its vision.

2014 — NEW MISSION/VISION
Environmental assessments show that the mission statement is ready for revision and that SDZG is ready for a new vision: to lead the fight against extinction.

2015 — LAUNCH OF THE CALL
The Call is a new strategic plan, created to focus SDZG on its new vision. It is a leaner, fully aligned plan with a much more ambitious goal.

Launching The Lynx

Once we had a vision, we knew where we wanted to go. And we had a strategic plan to help us get there—but The Lynx would require all our team members to work outside their comfort zone to improve key areas of the organization.

The Lynx strategic plan was a tough sell, though. It happened in the middle of an economic crisis, when people were worried about losing their jobs. To make matters worse, The Lynx represented compromise (which is often a first step toward fulfilling a long-term vision). Whether our staff members yearned for a conservation focus or they envisioned a future based on operational excellence, most weren't thrilled with the plan, but it was a necessary building block.

Fortunately, The Lynx had the support of our CEO and the VIS group. And instead of a binder full of spreadsheets like we had used in the past, The Lynx involved multifunctional teams of staff at all levels and trustees who were responsible for creating a structure of related actions. Each year, Doug and the VIS group reviewed the progress of The Lynx teams and held them accountable for their progress. Success was reported every month and—gradually—the organization came to see that Doug was serious about enacting change.

"Prior to The Lynx, plans went into a binder on the shelf," recalled Allison. "The Lynx was the first time we breathed life into our strategic plan."

Judy Kinsell, director of corporate and foundation relations, agreed. "Looking back at our last strategic plan of the 20th century, it reads like business as usual—a plan to do tomorrow what we are already doing today," she noted. "I think the biggest difference between then and now is that we realize we no longer have the luxury of doing tomorrow what we did today. The world is changing, animals in the wild are being slaughtered, and we have to rise up and make a difference because we can."

Interdepartmental Teamwork

As we worked toward our vision, we instituted three separate phases of The Lynx. Each phase lasted from three to four years and focused on different aspects of achieving the vision.

By far the most impactful—but painful—thing about The Lynx was the change to our internal culture. Previously, competition for scarce resources had turned our culture into a fiefdom, with every department a silo looking after itself. Even executives had become polarized within their business units when advocating for things like staffing, supplies, and funding.

The Lynx teams were tasked with fostering change that crossed departmental barriers. This went against the grain for many longtime employees, but over time, the silo mentality slowly gave way to a recognition that The Lynx couldn't be ignored, and the walls between departments began to come down.

During the three phases of The Lynx, four to six priority areas were established, with one team assigned to each area. Each team addressed the tactics (action items) for that year. For example, the first action item for "enhancing our interpretive efforts" was to assess our current interpretive efforts and compare them with best practices. The following year, the action item was to hire an interpretive manager; the third year, it was to develop an interpretive master plan, and so on. Teams were made up of staff from the Zoo, the Safari Park, and the Institute for Conservation Research. They were selected by the CEO and chief strategy officer and included a wide variety of skill sets, ages, and personality types. New teams were selected annually based on the tactics (action items) on The Lynx work plan for that year, with 40 to 50 people participating every year.

Many of the team members had never met before. Some had been on staff for years; others had just started. At first, some people resented The Lynx teams and carried on as usual, making unilateral decisions as soon as they returned to their home department. Gradually, though, they realized that the teams weren't going away and would be held accountable by the board and the CEO.

The Lynx teams forced people out of their comfort zone. Some fought back and some left the organization, replaced by new people who were excited by our shared goals. Fortunately, most were willing to adapt.

For instance, in one Lynx team meeting, the group had been asked to develop a process for ensuring the maintenance of old equipment. The process being considered was cumbersome and relied on input from many different departments. An operations manager jumped to his feet in frustration, knocking over his chair. "This is not how it's supposed to be!" he shouted. "We don't need a process for this! The general manager of the Zoo should be making these choices by himself!" He left the room, slamming the door on his way out.

He was right—in a perfect world, the general manager (GM) would have been making these decisions. But in our culture at that time, the GM was not getting the information he needed to make resource allocation decisions. The operations manager eventually cooled down. At the next team meeting, he helped the group make the process more manageable, and later, he even led his own Lynx team.

This emphasis on cross-functional, interdepartmental teams gradually chipped away at the departmental silos. Employees began requesting to be assigned to a Lynx team the following year, and the adversarial atmosphere at the executive level gradually developed into an alliance.

One of the standout employees was Dr. Bruce Rideout, director of disease investigations at SDZG, who led or participated in Lynx teams during all three phases of the plan. Bruce is a scientist who spends his days in the laboratory at the Institute for Conservation Research, but he was a master at challenging SDZG's long-held assumptions. He knew how to help a team get perspective about how its tasks related to the organization's vision.

"I was always amazed at what could happen when wildly divergent groups of people worked together on a shared goal," Bruce recalled. "I saw the most innovative ideas coming unexpectedly from young people in non-leadership positions, and sometimes the most stubborn and entrenched views came from leaders. But when they were brought together, magic would happen!"

Once, Bruce was on a Lynx team tasked with improving guest relations. The team members were discussing ways that they could meet guest expectations. "We'll never transform this organization if we just give people what they expect," said Bruce. "We have to give them something they never expected!" This shift in perspective helped the team think about guest relations from a different angle. One young woman on the team suggested having surprises around every corner for visitors: small, special moments of animal-keeper interaction that happened unexpectedly throughout the Zoo. The Zoo implemented the idea, and it became a great new way to connect guests with wildlife.

Changing Our Identity

One of the most pivotal decisions we made during The Lynx was to dramatically change our identity—something we knew was necessary to better connect people with wildlife. During the 20th century, the name of our parent organization, the Zoological Society of San Diego, had made sense. But it was not the name of a 21st-century company that had thousands of employees and conservation field projects on six continents. In 2010, we changed our name to San Diego Zoo Global, and almost immediately it resonated with the press and the public. In interviews or at cocktail parties, people would ask, "What does the 'global' part mean?" This gave us an opportunity to share our worldwide conservation story with everyone we encountered.

During The Lynx period, we also changed the name of the Zoo's sister facility, previously called the San Diego Wild Animal Park. While the 100-acre San Diego Zoo was world-famous, the 1,800-acre Wild Animal Park—just 30 miles away—was far less known, despite the fact that it could have held the entire San Diego Zoo in just one of its vast field enclosures. This amazing sanctuary, designed as a breeding facility, was home to entire herds of animals, such as elephants, giraffes, and many species of antelope. However, the Wild Animal Park had developed very little name recognition: the name was rather unwieldy and generic, and the general public had trouble remembering it. People also confused the Wild Animal Park with other Southern California wildlife parks.

Many guests who visited the Wild Animal Park were impressed by the wide-open field enclosures and herds of roaming animals, but they felt they did not need to return because they had "seen it all." The Wild Animal Park had never been designed to be profitable, but as time went by, the expense of operating it outpaced the revenue it generated. Of course, we still had to provide the same quality of animal care, nutrition, and veterinary services whether visitors came or not. This hampered our ability to thrive as an organization and to fulfill our vision at the time to "connect people with animals." As we homed in on the type of organization we wanted to become, we decided to change the Wild Animal Park's name to the San Diego Zoo Safari Park and rework its offerings to provide many different safari experiences that were both fun and repeatable.

It was a tough sell to those who loved the Wild Animal Park; many were afraid it would no longer be the unique, expansive experience it had always been. It quickly became clear, however, that it was the right choice. Within three years, the Safari Park had righted itself financially. Guests returned again and again to fly like a condor on our 2/3-mile zip line, ride in a caravan truck to feed giraffes and rhinos, spend the night at our Roar & Snore campsite, or enjoy one of our other safari experiences.

Reimagining the Volunteer Program

During The Lynx years, we also began to emphasize telling our stories. One great example of this was our reimagined volunteer program. For decades, a small band of dedicated volunteers had helped SDZG with special events, office work, and other back-of-house tasks. In 2008, our CEO, Doug Myers, and several board members visited other zoos across the country. "What struck us was that every zoo we visited had a pool of interpretive volunteers," recalled Berit Durler, former board chair and trustee emeritus.

Interpretive volunteers are trained to impart information to guests. SDZG had always steered clear of interpretive volunteers because we did not know how to ensure that unpaid volunteers would consistently provide high-quality, customer-friendly, factual information to our guests. As part of The Lynx, however, Berit and other board members insisted that we build our volunteer program to include interpretive training. The staff pushed back, concerned that we would be unable to implement a quality program. Berit, who was then president of the board, insisted. "We started with 300," Berit remembered. "Within a year we had a full cadre of volunteers."

To help implement this program—and our larger vision—we hired Tammy Rach as senior manager of volunteer services. She is a tireless advocate for the volunteers and has created programs for individualized training and evaluation for every volunteer. "We now have many interpretive volunteers who enhance the guest experience at both the Zoo and Safari Park," Tammy reported. "We also have people who chop hay daily for our elephant Mary and strip bamboo for giant panda Gao Gao's bamboo bread. Our volunteers created more than 25,500 enrichment items for animals in 2017. And that's just the tip of the iceberg!"

Since we overhauled the program in 2009, our volunteers have logged 1.6 million cumulative hours of service, a value estimated at more than $46 million. The volunteer program has grown to 2,000 community members who contribute 210,000 hours of service annually—the equivalent of 100 full-time staff members.

Like many elements of The Lynx, the volunteer program has expanded and improved during The Call. "In 2017, all of our active volunteers received additional training to become conservation ambassadors, learning about our conservation projects as well as how to incorporate The Call into their volunteer assignments," noted Tammy.

Innovative Storytelling

Another huge win during The Lynx years was the concept for The Harry and Grace Steele Elephant Odyssey complex at the San Diego Zoo. As part of our long-term facility plan, we were ready to renovate our elephant habitat to provide a much larger and more natural environment for the elephants. Our staff considered traditional ideas, such as talking about the land where the elephants originated, but we struggled with this concept because the elephants in our herd were from two different continents.

Ideas were swirling around about this new complex when the newly minted Interpretive Council (made up of both board and staff members) challenged the staff to come up with a concept that would tell an important story. The project team working on the elephant complex landed on an innovative idea: to tell the story of the elephants' relatives that had lived in Southern California during the Pleistocene epoch. The idea grew to include many animals and plants—sloths, tapirs, dung beetles, lions, jaguars, capybaras, condors, cycads, and more—that appeared to be unrelated but all had ancestors in Southern California sometime during the Pleistocene. The storytelling messages around this concept ranged from life in the Ice Age and the evolution of Southern California to current issues surrounding extinction and climate change.

When Elephant Odyssey opened, it told this story in many ways. Signage, statues, graphics, and other elements explained different facets of the Southern California historical thread that connected the animals and plants in the complex. Interpretive volunteers stationed at a simulated tar pit at the entrance showed fossils and replicas of extinct plants and animals to guests.

Elephant Odyssey became the most ambitious project that SDZG had undertaken at the time. It was many times more expensive than what we had originally planned—but as part of The Lynx, our organization was committed to attaining a leadership role in connecting people to wildlife and conservation.

"The Interpretive Council set this in motion," said Berit Durler. "We trusted the staff to come up with a unique concept. People started to feel that they had a voice. We told them, 'You can do this!' And the vision that they came up with for Elephant Odyssey is fabulous."

Setting the Stage

Each phase of The Lynx plan also moved our organization toward cross-functional, accountable teams and processes. "The three phases of The Lynx strategic plan allowed us to imagine The Call," said Dr. Bob Wiese, SDZG's chief life sciences officer. "We needed to grow to become a more strategic and focused organization. We broke down the walls within as well as the barriers going outward. This is what led to making The Call possible."

Not everything in The Lynx plans worked well. We had many bumps in the road: Staff members who had grown complacent were pushed out of their comfort zones. We made several attempts at implementing a process for recognizing internal innovation during The Lynx, but none of them took hold. We identified a process for resource allocation during the first phase of The Lynx that was eventually abandoned because it was too cumbersome. Each of these false starts helped us think about what was genuinely important to achieve our vision. If change was still necessary, we would regroup and try a different approach.

At times, The Lynx may have been hard to embrace due to its emphasis on accountability, processes, and positioning, but it was a terrific strategic plan, because it propelled us toward our goal. It taught us to focus on shared priorities as we never had before. In 2013, The Lynx won the coveted Goodman Award for Strategic Planning, the top honor from the Association of Strategic Planning.

Many of the key outcomes from the 10-year span that encompassed the three phases of The Lynx are mentioned throughout this book. Some were invisible but essential—internal adjustments that would allow for growth and help us determine how to allocate our limited resources to help wildlife. Here are some of the highlights.

- **We emphasized interpretation (telling our story internally and externally) by:**
  - Developing an interpretive master plan
  - Creating key messages, including the three crucial pieces of information that all guests should take away from their visit
  - Hiring an interpretive manager
  - Launching our first interpretive volunteer program
  - Changing our family of organizational identities to clarify the purpose and mission of each entity
  - Working to tell our conservation stories through public relations channels
- **We addressed foundational needs for an increasingly complex organization through:**
  - Shoring up internal decision-making processes
  - Creating alignment by providing shared goals and priorities
  - Developing HR processes, including staff satisfaction surveys, employee reviews, and increased accountability
- **We focused our conservation efforts by:**
  - Identifying our conservation niche
  - Creating a process to select conservation projects based on our conservation niche
  - Pulling conservation work together across many departments to get the best results from our conservation investments
  - Developing internal sustainability programs so we could "walk the talk"

Although the phases of The Lynx were not as inspiring as The Call, the original plans laid a foundation for future success. The Lynx forced us to examine how well we were inspiring others and helped us focus on becoming a world leader in connecting people to wildlife and conservation. Without The Lynx, many groups would not see us as a conservation organization today, and internally, we would not have organizational alignment about our vision.

When SDZG began to develop The Call, it stood on the shoulders of The Lynx. We could not have achieved transformational change toward becoming a conservation organization in 2002 and 2003, because we weren't ready—and the world wasn't ready—to think of SDZG as a conservation organization. "One of the things that has given The Call the power to be so transformational is how long we waited for it," noted Robin Keith, associate director of Vision, Innovation, and Strategy (VIS) for SDZG. "We wanted to be leaders in conservation for years before The Call, but we never could have realized that dream without the work we did in The Lynx years."

About "Simmering"

- Your group may have great ideas for the future, but it might not be ready to implement them. Use the information collected about your environment to decide if an idea is ahead of its time.
- Resist the impulse to plunge ahead with a good idea that does not have adequate support—instead, allow it to simmer until you can gain traction with key stakeholders.
- If the idea is worth pursuing but not immediately feasible, determine what steps you can take to position your organization to take advantage of the idea when the time is right.

Cliff Hague, a SDZG board member, agreed: "We realized we would have to completely rework our viewpoint if we were serious about transformative change. For many years, we talked about becoming a 'conservation zoo' and shifting our focus, but those in the operational areas of SDZG could not get their arms around how it would work from a business model perspective. Sometimes you have to let things simmer before you can see how they work. Staff may have to study and assess the viability of an idea before it can be accepted by the board."

By 2014, we realized that we had completed our vision of becoming a leader at connecting people to wildlife and conservation. We knew then that we were ready to take on a more ambitious vision—one that led to the birth of The Call.

CHAPTER

4

REMAINING NIMBLE IN A CHANGING WORLD

*"Happiness is when what you think, what you say,
and what you do are all in harmony."*
Mahatma Gandhi

One of the most valuable lessons we learned at San Diego Zoo Global was to adopt a continuous planning cycle. Previously, our strategic plans would last for a specified period of time. Each new planning period culminated in a plan . . . that sat on a shelf. Occasionally, we'd dust it off and assess our progress.

In the 21st century, we realized that the world was moving too fast to simply have a planning retreat every few years. Our strategy had to be adaptable and nimble—based on the realities of the day and in alignment between the plans and our execution of them. We needed to routinely scan our environment and measure our progress toward the vision. In short, we needed a new breed of strategic plan, one that was less of a binder on a shelf and more of a living document that kept us on our toes.

At first, as we began implementing The Lynx strategic plan, we moved too far in the opposite direction, changing our entire strategy on a dime in response to real-time environmental changes. We would set goals for the year, but a rainy first quarter could send us into a tailspin as we scrambled to make up for lost revenues. It confused the staff and volunteers, who felt that we were always moving the target. They didn't feel as though they were working toward a common goal. Instead, they felt like they were being handed a new set of priorities every day. This also left our organization too susceptible to overreacting to one strong voice or one environmental factor, rather than taking everything into account and seeing the big picture. It was impossible to align our resource allocation with our strategic plan.

Berit Durler, SDZG's former board chair and trustee emeritus, commented, "In the past, we had a five-year plan that was a tome. We spent so many hours creating it, and then it went on the shelf. Eventually, we went from a five-year plan to an authentic strategic planning cycle, and it made all the difference."

A New Timeline

In effect, we realized that transformational results would require a decade or more of concerted effort and an organizational commitment. How could we make meaningful, lasting change if the target was always shifting?

We also recognized that we must employ multiple time horizons. This was a key differentiator for The Lynx. By creating clear boundaries, we could remain both agile *and* committed.

Here is the continuous cycle of planning that we employed at SDZG:

Mission, vision, and values: Every seven to 10 years

We thoroughly examined the mission, vision, and values of our organization during this time frame, whether we felt the need for it or not.

Our Lynx-era vision statement—to become a world leader at connecting people to wildlife and conservation—represented an achievement. Unlike our mission and values, which were guidelines to provide direction moving forward, our vision represented the future that we had selected.

We found that a vision statement should encompass seven to 10 years of focused work. A vision that could be completed in a shorter time was less likely to be transformational, whereas a vision that entailed more than 10 years of effort would be hard to sustain, requiring reimagining or at least renewed focus. During this time, we constantly measured progress toward our vision, but after seven to 10 years of implementing The Lynx, we were ready to start looking ahead to a new vision: The Call.

Strategic priorities and strategies: Every three to five years

This represented the hardest time horizon to adhere to. Inevitably, unforeseen opportunities would present themselves, tempting us to change focus. However, we could never hit a moving target, so we needed to leave our core strategies in place for three to five years, barring a drastic shift (for better or worse) in environmental factors.

Although we changed how we implemented these strategies annually through our operational plan, we kept the high-level strategies consistent to ensure all eyes remained focused on the vision. At first, we worried that our organization would not remain flexible if we left these strategies in place, but we came to appreciate they were a crucial building block to bringing our vision to life.

Each of our Lynx strategic plans took about three years to complete. Our vision lasted through all three phases of The Lynx.

Operation plan (tactics): Every year

Our tactics and annual action items were intended to last only a year and were tied to our annual budget. This was the level at which we could remain flexible and adjust as needed to take advantage of windfalls or to dodge pitfalls.

For SDZG, it was imperative to keep our tactics firmly under the umbrella of our key strategies, or we would risk veering off course. Sticking to the cycle allowed us to achieve the most influence, but changing our tactics annually positioned us to leverage opportunities as they came up.

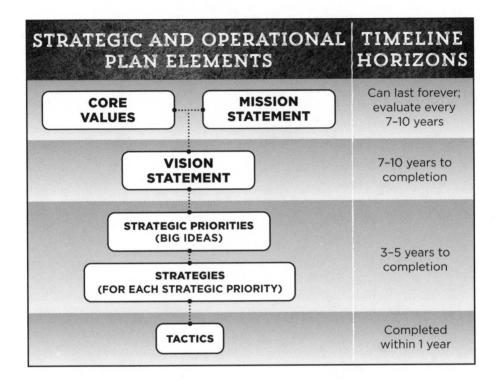

Overall, we learned that creating a strategic planning and implementation cycle with multiple time horizons allowed us to work continually toward our desired future. This was a key differentiator from both our old-school plans—which remained static—and the current tendency for organizations to switch everything based on the daily weather report. With clarity around these boundaries, we found it was possible to adhere to multiple time horizons and remain both agile and committed. In fact, our commitment to this cycle provided the rigor that allowed us to achieve even bigger dreams.

ADOPTING A FACILITATIVE APPROACH

"If you had to identify, in one word, the reason why the human race has not achieved—and never will achieve—its full potential, that word would be meetings."

Dave Barry, author and humorist

One of the key elements that helped transform San Diego Zoo Global was our decision to adopt a facilitative approach. In 2001, CEO Doug Myers created the Vision, Innovation, and Strategy (VIS) group, tasking its members with overseeing the organization's strategic planning processes and serving as organizational facilitators. These individuals enhanced group success by helping to improve decision-making, productivity, and problem-solving. They brought people together, guided the process, and followed up to ensure that all outcomes were met. In fact, every meeting referenced in this book was facilitated by someone from VIS.

Rather than have facilitators who were committed to remaining neutral and simply devoted to keeping a group on task and on time, Doug envisioned something more. He wanted strategic facilitators who were "internal consultants"—employees who would help groups solve organization-wide problems by using a consultative viewpoint. Instead of staying neutral, these strategic facilitators would get involved because they would see the entire organization as their "client." This would ensure that each group's work was informed by the larger goals of the organization as well as by the work of other internal groups.

The VIS facilitators also helped Doug make the best use of his time. In the past, Doug lacked adequate time to engage in leadership functions because he was so busy attending meetings. He had a monthly board meeting, a monthly board committee meeting, impromptu meetings with board members, evening events with members and donors, and other meetings with staff. In short, he spent the vast majority of his time simply attending meetings.

Once Doug began to include VIS facilitators in more and more key meetings to ensure that the meeting outcomes were met, he was freed up to listen, ponder, and participate without being forced to referee. Ultimately, almost every internal board or executive meeting was guided by one of these strategic facilitators.

It might seem that having professional facilitators at every key meeting is a luxury few nonprofits could afford, but these facilitators provided a positive return on both investment and mission. They insisted on concrete outcomes and proactive planning; they invited the right people for a discussion; and they aligned the organization with our strategies. All of this saved the organization time and money—in addition to keeping a laser focus on our vision.

Strategic Facilitation Steps

Over time, the VIS strategic facilitation team found that these steps added the most value to a group's process. For each meeting, the facilitators:

- **Clarified meeting roles and expectations prior to the meeting.** Before a meeting started, the facilitators found out whether everyone had an equal role or if some group members had specific roles. This was crucial: sometimes, a leader would expect subordinates to speak up, but the employees were under the impression that they were meant only to observe. This was not something we wanted to hash out during valuable meeting time.

- **Matched their methods to the meeting.** Some types of meetings were enhanced by technological solutions; for other meetings, technology was a distraction. If the expected outcome of a meeting was for participants to learn something new, then a computer presentation (projected or sent to the group members' devices) or virtual meeting might be in order. If the expected outcome was to discuss a controversial subject, however, the group would benefit most from a face-to-face meeting in a well-lit room with maximum eye contact. In those cases, the facilitators would go low-tech with a whiteboard, flip chart, or printed handouts.

- **Specified an outcome for every agenda item.** This ensured that we continued to move things forward. Otherwise, our meetings could result in nothing more than a decision to schedule another meeting! Having specific outcomes for each agenda item also allowed the participants to pace themselves and to see which part of the agenda would be best to bring up issues of concern. As we discovered, people are more likely to work within the meeting's framework if they understand how and when their topics will be addressed.

- **Determined a decision-making model in advance.** Each group made decisions in various ways, but the facilitators clarified our method in advance of the group's first meeting. (For example, groups governed by a charter might require a motion followed by a vote, while informal groups usually prefer consensus.) Our facilitators also found it useful to have a plan for what to do if the method we selected couldn't be achieved. In that case, would a leader make the decision? Surprisingly, the threat of having a leader decide worked well: sometimes, team members chose to negotiate rather than defer decision-making power to someone else.

- **Set (and enforced) meeting-specific ground rules.** The facilitators set rules specific to the group dynamic, such as the decision-making model, parameters for time, use of electronic devices, and expectations for confidentiality or information sharing between meetings. It was important for the facilitators to hold their groups accountable, as participants took their cue from the facilitator about whether the rules would be enforced.

- **Engaged all participants from the beginning of the meeting.** The VIS facilitators understood that some participants would feel uncomfortable at the outset. Maybe certain participants didn't know many attendees, they were worried about possible outcomes, or they didn't completely understand their role. In meetings where this dynamic was present, the facilitators began with an activity that required everyone to engage. This ensured they would all see themselves as participants instead of outsiders. One of the most useful activities was to simply give everyone a chance to go around the room, identify themselves, and answer a relevant question such as, "What would a successful meeting look like from your vantage point?" By the time everyone replied, they felt like they were a genuine part of the group and had something valuable to contribute. This also allowed the facilitator to gently redirect any expectations for an outcome not listed on the agenda.

- **Ensured that both introverts and extroverts could contribute.** Brainstorming is a great way to get a lot of ideas quickly, and discussions are good for finding out how various participants look at the sides of an issue. Both of these popular agenda items rely on verbal expression, though, and the VIS facilitators found that the extroverts in the meetings tended to participate in these activities more often. So the facilitators looked for ways to ensure that the introverts in the room could give their best input too. When dealing with high-stakes issues, the facilitators tried to provide everyone enough time to write down their ideas or to participate via an electronic poll.

- **Allowed time for an honorable close.** When we were crunched for time to get through a meeting, the conclusion was usually the part that got an abrupt end. In dealing with high-stakes topics or a high level of disagreement, however, it was essential to end the meeting with a short check-in. The facilitators asked, "Did everyone achieve the outcomes they agreed to at the beginning of the meeting?" If so, it would be hard for any of the participants to grumble about the outcome outside the meeting. If not, the facilitators made notes of anything the group members weren't satisfied with—and how these would be addressed going forward.

- **Ensured that we had the right environment for success.** Every meeting setup has pros and cons, but physical factors are often overlooked. For instance, SDZG held one daylong meeting with 20 participants in a beautiful hotel boardroom with a gorgeous view of the city. The room was equipped with all the latest technology and featured a polished mahogany table that seated exactly 20 people—without an inch between the chairs. The agenda called for an activity that required the group members to move around the room, but the participants had to turn sideways to squeeze their way out of their seats. Everyone felt cramped and crabby that day, inhibiting any innovative ideas the group may have had.

Freeing Up Time to Be Strategic

In addition to running important meetings, our VIS facilitators helped oversee the board's new committees. In 2003, Doug worked with then-board chair Yvonne Larsen to overhaul the board committee and meeting system. They kept the board committees that were required by the bylaws, but in place of the other committees, they formed a small number of board and staff advisory councils. It was a hard transition. The members of the former committees had been invited to join those groups for life, and many were disappointed to see them end—but it was essential for SDZG to implement real, lasting change.

Doug asked the VIS group members to help oversee the formation of these new councils. They created charters for the groups by bringing board leaders and staff leaders together to ensure alignment with our strategic plan (at the time, The Lynx). Instead of meeting every month, these councils met only when something truly required discussion, so staff members were relieved of their commitment to create monthly show-and-tell presentations. To energize the councils with fresh thinking, the charters were updated and membership rotated each year.

As they did with staff meetings, the VIS facilitators kept these council meetings firmly on track. This sometimes created frustration for participants who felt constrained by the charters, the strategic plan, and the clock. Gradually, though, the expectation was set: group members realized that the meetings would be guided by the organization's overall goals, with tight agendas, solid outcomes, and a hard stop at the appointed ending time.

It took a team effort to bring forth these changes. Doug was motivated to find a more productive use of time for himself and his board members, and he was willing to put his faith in the strategic facilitation process. The board, under strong leadership, was willing to try something new after years of stasis. And the VIS group remained adaptable, tweaking the process and facilitation as the players and goals shifted over the years.

Facilitation and Collaboration

In time, this facilitative approach took on a much bigger role. The board and staff leaders realized that if the right strategies and meeting management could transform SDZG, then these services would help the entire field of animal and plant conservation.

Soon, our VIS group conducted many high-stakes strategic planning processes and facilitated crucial meetings for SDZG's collaborators. These included strategic plans for organizations and associations such as the Association of Zoos and Aquariums, the Charles Darwin Foundation in Ecuador, the Alliance for Sustainable Wildlife, the Balboa Park Cultural Partnership, the Center for Plant Conservation, and a collaborative group dedicated to saving all the native wildlife across the continent of Australia. VIS also facilitated meetings of conservation groups around key topics, such as animal welfare, disease risk assessments, and creating multiorganizational conservation plans for endangered animals.

One important collaborator for us was the American Alliance of Museums (AAM).[11] In 2008, AAM was upside-down financially. Many organizations found it difficult to reach their budget goals during the financial crisis. But AAM—a membership organization for museums—was hit particularly hard, as the growing popularity of networking technology and the economic woes of its member museums undercut AAM's value proposition. Despite the efforts of AAM's dedicated staff, budget cuts forced layoffs for the association, and one museum was closing every month across the country.

SDZG CEO Doug Myers was the vice-chair of the AAM board. As the incoming president of the board, Doug was assigned to create a strategic plan to help AAM, so he brought in someone from VIS to create a transformational plan for the association. In 2009, the board hired a new CEO, Dr. Ford W. Bell, who was committed to changing the tide. Under AAM's resulting strategic plan, the organization would have to make key changes: a commitment to financial sustainability, a more accessible accreditation process, and strong advocacy for the museum field at state and local levels.

At first, staff members found it difficult to get behind the new plan, but eventually they began to think of exciting possibilities for change. VIS continued to work with AAM at both the board and staff levels. AAM branded the new plan "The Spark" and began to include it in the association's daily culture. Meanwhile, Doug insisted that every AAM board meeting include reports on key elements of The Spark, and a new CFO, Laura Lott, was recruited to oversee the financial sustainability of the organization.

AAM's strategic plan aimed to completely revamp the association's membership model. The board held a retreat (facilitated by VIS) in San Diego to discuss this goal. At the retreat, board member Dr. John Wetenhall—president of the Carnegie Museums of Pittsburgh—commented, "We are asking exactly the wrong question. The right question is, how do we *double* or *triple* membership? Do we want incremental change or systemic change? What difference is 1 or 2 percent more members going to have on this organization?"

Wetenhall's big question resonated with the group members. They asked, "How do we make AAM membership a necessity and not an option?" Once the question had been framed, AAM realized what needed to happen. The association flipped its membership model upside-down, with a new tiered membership paradigm that addressed the needs of the museums. In less than a year, the team had revamped the program, rebranded AAM, and rebuilt the technology infrastructure.

By 2012, AAM was operating in the black after four consecutive years of losing money. By 2013, the association netted $530,000—its biggest surplus in a decade. And by 2014, its membership increased by 34 percent . . . not only reversing a dozen years of decline but also setting a new record.

The Spark didn't make this turnaround; like The Lynx and The Call, AAM's plan simply helped the staff, the board, and its leaders see a light at the end of the tunnel and provided a map to get there.

About the Facilitative Approach

SDZG uses a facilitative approach for our conservation work. This approach helps us to solve large-scale issues for endangered species by bringing collaborators together, agreeing on outcomes, identifying roles, and following up.

The facilitative approach can benefit any organization.

- Facilitators enhance group success by helping to improve decision-making, productivity, and problem-solving. They bring people together, guide the process, and follow up to ensure that all outcomes have been met.
- Facilitators also ensure meetings are outcome driven. They carefully consider the meeting dynamics, including the environment, methods, participation, risk level, and roles.

CREATING
THE CALL

IDENTIFYING OUR
CORE VALUES

"It's not hard to make decisions once you know what your values are."
Roy E. Disney

As San Diego Zoo Global began the strategic planning cycle, we knew it was important to identify the elements to keep before we could decide what to change. So we employed a multidepartmental, multilevel effort to brainstorm organizational values and identify what made SDZG tick. We resisted the temptation to restate the mission or create a list of platitudes that could apply to any organization, instead pushing ourselves to think deeply about what convictions made our organization unique.

As a staff, we weren't always good at implementing these principles. For instance, we wrestled with the value of "working together." We knew it was essential and that we could achieve so much more if we came together. But this was not our strong suit. At the time that we identified our values, we were stuck in departmental silos and did not always play well with others. Nonetheless, we knew we were stronger together and that unity was important for overall success . . . so we valued this trait, even when we struggled to bring it to life.

For this reason, we didn't identify values that we would like the organization to have; instead, we uncovered the beliefs that had always existed at SDZG. We pushed ourselves to find the tenets that were so embedded in the organization that we would still hold to them even if they became a disadvantage for us. True core values don't change over the lifetime of an organization, regardless of changes in leadership, personnel, and environmental factors.

It was hard to synthesize the principles that were key to the culture, but the process was beneficial. Ted Molter, SDZG's chief marketing officer, was a key leader of this process. He recalled that we started the effort by trying to ensure the values felt right to all participants. "I wondered, 'How do we make sure everyone wins in this?'" said Ted. "But I quickly realized that rather than having the group choose the principles that each member liked the best, the values had to emerge on their own."

Ted continued, "The fact that they've stood the test of time shows that we got it right." The team worked hard to ensure that the wording best represented SDZG's personality: "Obviously, sustainable financial success is important to our organization—that keeps it going. And by choosing the wording 'breed financial stability,' we made it specific to SDZG. This wording helped to clarify that the funding we received would be used to help animals."

Ted also liked the last line of SDZG's core values: "Remember the roar and pass it on." He said, "I felt that it was the perfect finishing touch."

SDZG's Core Values

Listed here are SDZG's core values, entitled The Roar:

* **Make a difference for wildlife.** Everyone's job contributes to the well-being of plants, animals, and ecosystems here and around the world. For some, the connection is direct—they are doing field conservation, caring for plants and animals, or developing animal diets. The rest of us feel a great sense of pride and satisfaction in the knowledge that our

jobs sustain this vital work. Whenever possible, we inspire people to take action to help wildlife.

- **Share the wonder of nature.** Whatever job we do, we are passionate about introducing others to the beauty and mystery of the natural world. We are dedicated to providing the most outstanding wildlife experience for our guests and sharing our discoveries with our colleagues. We enjoy celebrating the wonder of nature with the world.

- **Feel the passion for what we do.** Our employees share a zeal for the mission of this organization, along with a great sense of pride about the nobility of our work. We value the individual energy that makes this place great, which manifests itself in the drive to champion a project and see it through to completion. Because much of our work is highly specialized, we are constantly striving to ensure that we are a part of things, that our voices are heard, and that our expertise is sought after.

- **Breed financial stability.** We recognize that financial stability is vital to our success. We use sound business practices to make strategic decisions about how our financial resources will be allocated. We actively seek new financial opportunities to maximize the value of our assets. We share a sense of perspective that helps us discern what is truly important, and we have the integrity to do the right thing.

- **Succeed together.** The unique dynamics of this organization and this industry make collaboration a challenge, yet we recognize that ultimately we are all working toward the same common goals. We steadfastly support that which we've created, and this leads to a sense of shared purpose that extends to all areas of the organization, as well as local, national, and world communities. We share a can-do spirit and an excitement about new opportunities. We feel a sense of responsibility for the success of the entire organization, so we openly offer and receive feedback. We recognize that working together—as coworkers, conservation collaborators, business partners, and colleagues—produces synergistic benefits that exceed the value of what we can each accomplish alone.

- **Remember the roar . . . and pass it on.** We have enjoyed a reputation for creative problem-solving since the days of our founder, Dr. Harry Wegeforth. We share a dedication to discovery—of new situations, new opportunities, and new ways to work—that will live up to the world's expectations of us. We celebrate our unique organizational heritage, and we are committed to leaving a legacy for those who follow us.

These values have become the criteria for recognizing exceptional employees at SDZG. Managers can recommend their staff members for internal awards by citing examples of how they represent one of the core values in The Roar. Our values are also used in recruitment, to attract potential employees who connect with our tenets.

Most importantly, these values will last throughout the life of our organization. They may be reworded or others added, but regardless of how they're identified, these core tenets have always been important to SDZG and always will be—long after the current board members and staff leaders have all retired.

Remembering the Roar

What exactly is "the roar"? This core value is an integral part of our story, referring to the founding of the San Diego Zoo more than a century ago.

On September 26, 1916, Dr. Harry Wegeforth, a local physician, was driving back to his San Diego office with his brother, Paul, after performing surgery. As they drove past Balboa Park, Dr. Harry heard a lion roaring. Dr. Harry had always had an interest in animals, so he turned to his brother and said, "Wouldn't it be splendid if San Diego had a zoo? You know . . . I think I'll start one."

About Core Values

- Values are the core tenets of an organization.
- Values—properly identified—should not change, even when the organizational leadership changes.
- Values are not aspirational; they represent what is important to your organization, not principles you are striving for.
- An organization's values and mission form the ground floor upon which the vision and strategies are built.

The roaring lion was one of the animals that had been left from the 1915–16 Panama-California Exposition, which had closed earlier that year. The exposition was meant to celebrate the opening of the Panama Canal and to put the city of San Diego on the map. It was an elaborate World's Fair–style event, with dozens of new buildings, exhibits that represented places around the world, and one-of-a-kind experiences—some that included wild animals. At the close of the exposition, the company in charge of the animal exhibits had left. Just a few caretakers remained. Wolves, coyotes, bears, monkeys, and the roaring lion all lived in cages along the side of the street. Another part of the exposition held bison, elk, and deer. The city was reluctantly in charge of the animals, but its managers were looking for another option.

Initially, the community thought "Dr. Harry," as he came to be known, was a fool for trying to create a world-class zoo in a city of only 40,000 people. People assumed the idea of a zoo was a joke, calling it "Wegeforth's Folly." But Dr. Harry was determined. It was his enthusiasm, confidence, charm, and skill—combined with a good measure of stubborn persistence—that set it all in motion. He had a vision from the beginning, and he stepped up to say that he would assume responsibility for the animals, founding the

Zoological Society of San Diego one week later (October 2, 1916).

More than a century later, San Diego Zoo employees still tell this story and marvel at how far the organization has come. The value "remember the roar and pass it on" speaks to this legacy, as well as the commitment to keeping it alive for generations to come. As Ted pointed out, "History and longevity are core underpinnings of our culture. We celebrate longevity as well as a passion for animals and plants. I remember the roar, and so does everyone else at SDZG."

EXAMINING OUR MISSION

*"A mission statement is not something you write overnight, but
fundamentally, your mission statement becomes your constitution, the
solid expression of your vision and values. It becomes the criterion by
which you measure everything else."*
Stephen Covey, author

At San Diego Zoo Global, we believe that our values and mission statement are the heart of our organization. While our value statements express the principles that are important to us, our mission statement explains what our organization is and what it does. It helps us to separate our work from that of others with a similar cause and to clarify the scope of our organization's purpose.

Over time, we have found:

- **Mission statements are not wishful thinking.** Our mission statement explains what we do, not what we plan to do. While our vision is aspirational, our mission statement is not.

- **Mission statements do not need to list every single thing that an organization does.** Our organizational mission highlights the higher-level concept of our scope of activities, but it does not describe every way in which we might possibly deliver on this. It is an umbrella for everything that fits underneath . . . but it also has clear edges to help us see what does not fit under the umbrella.

- **Mission statements are not meant to be updated frequently.** The purpose of an organization should not change very often. In fact, many organizations keep the same mission statement throughout the entire life cycle of the company. However, if SDZG changes an important component, we revise our mission statement. We believe our mission should be reviewed every few years as part of SDZG's strategic planning cycle to ensure that it is still relevant and aligned with the other parts of our strategic plan.

Identifying Our New Mission Statement

For decades, our mission statement had been: "The San Diego Zoo is a conservation, education, and recreation organization dedicated to the reproduction, protection, and exhibition of animals, plants, and their habitats." In the abstract, we viewed conservation, education, and recreation as representing three equal parts of our organization, using a three-legged stool as the visual embodiment of our mission, with each leg crucial to keep the stool upright. In practice, though, we had many disagreements about how to support each element of our identity. Departments felt that they fell under one leg or another, which inhibited cross-departmental collaboration. As our organization became more and more divided about whether our primary purpose was to entertain guests, educate the public, or conserve wildlife, our discussions about the three-legged stool became more and more heated.

In 2013, we solicited input about our mission statement from all SDZG board members, volunteers, and staff. We asked them, "Why does SDZG exist? What purpose does it serve?" Overwhelmingly, the answers centered around conservation of animals and plants. We also asked, "What is the current mission statement of SDZG?" Most could not recall the statement; others remembered only the words "conservation, education, and recreation." Overwhelmingly, however, our responders felt that SDZG had become a conservation organization.

We overlaid these survey comments with the data we had collected during our most recent environmental scan to ensure that we were using facts to back up our feelings. A market research poll by Harris Interactive had shown that the public now saw us as a conservation organization too—and the timing was more urgent than ever. Biodiversity loss was not slowing down. Zoos needed to "walk the talk" regarding conservation. It would no longer be enough to simply educate people about conservation; we had to shift our focus and make sure all our goals and priorities were truly aligned as a conservation organization.

Next, our executive team reviewed the results of the mission survey alongside the environmental scans. While the team members felt we could consider ourselves a conservation organization, they were concerned how this would be reflected in our mission. They wondered, "How could our mission focus solely on conservation without de-emphasizing the importance of the animals and plants in our care?"

As the executive team members discussed the issue, they realized that we were delivering on our conservation mission by unifying our efforts to care for plants and animals, inspire empathy for wildlife, and employ a scientific approach to conservation issues. The new mission would showcase all the ways in which staff and volunteers were already contributing to our reason for existing.

A small band of wordsmiths turned the executive team's concepts into a statement that would provide SDZG with direction. Then CEO Doug Myers presented the statement to the board members, who unanimously accepted the mission. Approved that same year, the new mission statement focused on conservation: "We are committed to saving species worldwide by uniting our expertise in animal care and conservation science with our dedication to inspiring passion for nature."

Eventually, SDZG dropped the concept of the three-legged stool, as our overarching concern for saving species made it irrelevant. "Replacing the three-legged stool of conservation, education, and recreation was one of the most pivotal moments in our strategic progress," observed Dr. Allison Alberts. "The stool analogy had caused us problems for years because it was divisive—departments were perceived as being linked to one leg of the stool or another, and we pitted them against each other in competition for resources. It encapsulated what had been wrong with our organization: the silo mentality and the idea that only one department at SDZG 'owned' each leg. We had to get a new mission statement to finally jettison this model."

Our *Why*

The new mission put the focus squarely on the animals and better reflected what we were already doing to help conserve wildlife around the world. For example, SDZG works with many partners to help save elephants and other animals in Kenya, where African elephants are threatened by poaching, human-wildlife conflict, and human-caused activities—practices that are continuing at unsustainable rates. Fortunately, community-driven conservation efforts in a remote section of the country are having a significant impact. This area is home to Kenya's second-largest elephant population and includes an elephant orphanage that is owned by the community. The people who share the land with the elephants provide the extended care that the calves need until they are weaned at around two or three years of age. Then the calves are released back to native elephant herds. As a result, the number of illegally killed elephants in these community conservancies has decreased by 53 percent over the past five years.

Conservation efforts like this constitute our *why*. Identifying our *why*—that is, figuring out why we do what we do—was one of the hardest and yet most important parts of developing our mission statement.

Many organizations struggle with finding their *why*. In his book *Start with Why*, Simon Sinek talks about a paradigm shift that he uncovered in his quest to find out why some organizations were exponentially more innovative and influential than others.[12] He identified a "golden circle" that contains the *what*, *how*, and *why* of a company's reason for being. Sinek came to realize that almost every organization knows what they do. Some organizations can describe how they do it. But few organizations can clearly articulate the reason why.

After decades of splitting our attention between conservation, education, and recreation, we were relieved to identify our *why*. For SDZG, it became abundantly clear that the reason we exist is to help save animal and plant species from extinction.

About Mission Statements

- A mission statement identifies the purpose of an organization. It is a succinct sentence that states an organization's broad scope of activities, its intended beneficiaries, its reason for existing, and the points that differentiate the company from similar organizations.
- A mission statement should have a long life span. It should only be changed when some key component of the business is altered.
- Unlike other parts of a strategic plan, a mission statement is not aspirational. It explains what you do, not what you have planned.

IMAGINING A BOLD FUTURE

*"The greatest danger for most of us is not that our aim is too high and
we miss it, but that it is too low and we reach it."*
Michelangelo

The best possible future for any organization is the one that is compelling, backed up by solid facts and information, goal-oriented, and supports a sustainable business model. After San Diego Zoo Global had undertaken our first-ever visioning process back in 2001, we were forced to take a hard look at what we wanted to achieve. While many of us hoped to become a major conservation nongovernmental organization (NGO), our first environmental assessment showed that at the time we would not be able to pull this off. So we invested 10 years of concentrated effort in the direction of our dreams, and by 2011, we were ready to wrap up The Lynx and take the next step.

It was one thing to think about moving to a new vision, but it was another thing to consider how we would agree on a shared future. While our vision for The Lynx had been meaningful, it had been hard to agree on and even harder to live out. Wouldn't the next vision be just as difficult to craft—or worse?

Fortunately, it was nothing like our previous vision process because we had carefully positioned ourselves for the next step. First, we considered the many paths our organization could take. We started with the most obvious one: stay on the current trajectory, streamlining processes and improving outcomes. Then we thought about other paths. We asked, "What opportunities did we uncover in the environmental scan phase? What legal challenges on the horizon will require us to adapt our current business model? What ideas have we heard from our stakeholders?" We listed all the possibilities, even those that seemed too far afield, too expensive, or too risky.

Armed with these ideas, our executive staff planned a retreat at a nearby hotel to ponder potential visions. Mark Stuart, SDZG's chief development and membership officer, was deep in thought as he drove to the hotel. He recalled all the work the team had done on SDZG's previous vision. Then he thought about a recent conference he had attended. There, author and fundraising consultant Simone Joyaux had said, "Donors give through your organization to achieve their own desires, to express their own values. Putting the donor in the center of the relationship, or being donor-centered, means focusing on meeting donors' needs rather than the needs of the organization."[13]

Mark's takeaway was that a nonprofit is not in business to be needy—instead, it is in business to solve a community need. Mark was pondering this as he pulled into the hotel parking garage. He locked his car and walked to the elevator. Just as the elevator doors began to close, he saw a minivan with a bumper sticker that said, "Kill cancer."

The phrase "kill cancer" stuck in his head. When he arrived at the retreat, he shared it with the other staff leaders. "Who doesn't want to kill cancer?" Mark asked. "You don't have to explain why you need to kill cancer or how you're going to do it. You just need to crystallize your cause to get people on board. It needs to be that simple."

The Moment Everything Changed

During the planning activities, Mark's "kill cancer" example was on everyone's mind. The executive staff had already synthesized our internal and external environmental factors at a previous meeting, and they were ready to move to the next level. It became clear that the responsible path for SDZG was to work to lead the fight against extinction—in fact, this became our new vision. While the group knew we could not possibly end extinction by working alone, they also understood—via our environmental assessment—that our organization was uniquely suited to take a leadership role. SDZG was well positioned to coordinate our partners to work together toward saving species. Quickly, the executive staff realized that "End extinction!" must become our rallying cry.

All at once, the group fell silent.

"It was just so crystal clear that it was the right thing for us to pursue," remembered Paula Brock, SDZG's chief financial officer. "I've never participated in any group planning effort where the answer came to us and immediately stuck. It represented the essence of what we were hoping to do, striving to do. It was clear—yet difficult—and achievable. After 97 years as an organization, we had been traveling along a path to get to that moment of convergence and unity. We're quite a diverse group of people, yet we all looked around and there was no argument."

Dr. Bob Wiese, SDZG's chief life sciences officer, agreed: "We ended up with a spectacular vision. It was so lofty and so audacious—yet so necessary for the fate of animal and plant species. As soon as we heard it, we knew it was right for us."

The next step was for CEO Doug Myers to carry this vision to the board of trustees and get their thoughts. The board and staff at SDZG have always wrestled with a healthy tension between various goals, and Doug knew he would have his hands full in explaining the new vision to the board. While the executive staff members had the benefit of realizing the vision all at once, the board would be hearing it after the fact. Nonetheless, Doug believed strongly that the vision was on target.

In his presentation to the board, Doug shared the metrics that indicated SDZG's previous vision had been achieved. He showed the board how crucial it was for animal and plant species to be recovered from the brink of extinction. Perhaps most importantly, he demonstrated how the San Diego Zoo and San Diego Zoo Safari Park could become two sanctuaries that not only educated the public but also contributed to SDZG's conservation efforts. And it worked.

"It was truly a 'eureka moment' for all of us," recalled one of our board members, Cliff Hague. "We immediately realized that we needed to stand our vision on its head and reverse it. We could no longer be a zoological garden that implemented conservation projects; instead, we became—in that moment—a conservation organization that ran a zoo, a safari park, and an institute for conservation research. The recreation elements we were implementing became the mechanisms by which the vision would be achieved, and now these elements would be evaluated in the context of the vision. It was so timely that it achieved instant universal acceptance by the board. Everyone felt it simultaneously. We all had goosebumps."

Cliff was not the only one to describe this physical response to the vision. Board member Dr. Linda Lowenstine recalled, "When I first heard the new vision, it gave me chills of joy to think about the ramifications and the future possibilities for our organization."

Another board member, Javade Chaudhri, put it this way: "When I first arrived at SDZG, there were people who said, 'Conservation is important, but what we need to do is to provide animals on exhibit to make money, and we can't mess with that formula.' In the finest traditions of honoring our history, and in no way denigrating it, we accepted the fact that we were smart enough to change for the sake of these endangered species."

About Vision Statements

- A vision statement is an organization's chosen future.
- A vision should be aspirational. It should take at least seven to 10 years to achieve through diligent effort and focus.
- The best possible future for any organization is the one that is the most compelling; the one that is backed up by solid facts and information; the one that is a stretch, but achievable; and the one that supports a sustainable business model.
- A crucial step for a planning team is to explore the implications of each potential vision to make sure the team doesn't move forward with a concept that it does not fully understand or cannot support.

DETERMINING OUR PRIORITIES

"When everything is a priority, nothing is a priority."
Karen Martin, author

Most people don't like to prioritize because it means choosing one thing over another. At San Diego Zoo Global, our choices can be particularly heartbreaking because they often force us to help one animal instead of another.

Dr. Nadine Lamberski, SDZG chief animal health officer, knows a lot about the sacrifices of prioritization. She recalled an incident in 2017 when the US Fish and Wildlife Service contacted SDZG regarding an endangered tiger cub confiscated at the border between the United States and Mexico. Border inspectors found the cub lying on the floor in the front seat of a car as smugglers attempted to enter the United States. The cub weighed only six pounds, and our animal care team estimated that he was about five or six weeks old. With his oversized paws and hoarse little growls, he was extremely cute and cuddly.

It sounds like an obvious fit. The tiger needed a home, and the Safari Park had an expansive, new tiger enclosure just 40 miles north of the border. But as Nadine understood, taking in that tiger would require resources that had already been allocated elsewhere. It would require prioritizing that tiger's needs over the needs of other animals.

SDZG is often asked to take in wild animals—mammals, birds, and reptiles—that are brought illegally into the United States. "We want to help all of them," Nadine said, "but we don't always have the space and animal care expertise necessary to provide for their well-being."

When we take in a confiscated animal, it is kept in quarantine for approximately 30 days to ensure it is healthy and does not introduce any disease to other animals. Every confiscation leads to a series of questions that must be answered. Nadine explained, "We have to ask, 'Do we have quarantine space available?' 'Does the animal come with health problems that would require extensive veterinary work?' 'Will we have enough personnel and resources to provide for the animal's veterinary care, daily care, and nutritional needs?' 'Will we have adequate space to house the animal comfortably as it grows?' 'If the animal requires socialization, will we be able to house it with other members of its species?'"

Most of all, choosing to take in a confiscated animal requires us to say no to something else. "We are committed to providing every animal in our care with the best life possible," Nadine said. "We can't take in an animal that would cause us to compromise the care of the animals we already have."

After we evaluated the situation, we decided we could care for the confiscated cub at the Safari Park, at least temporarily. The tiger cub, named Moka, was paired with another cub whose mother had failed to care for it, a critically endangered Sumatran tiger cub named Rakan. The two cubs grew up together. While Rakan can eventually become part of SDZG's breeding program to help save his species, Moka will not be eligible to participate in a breeding program because he is a hybrid of several different tiger subspecies. He received a permanent home at a local wildlife rescue facility.

Stories like this are part and parcel of saving endangered animals and plants. It can be gut-wrenching to try to decide how to allocate scarce resources and whether to focus on individuals or an entire species. We knew that if we were to achieve our dream of leading the fight against extinction, our strategic plan needed to provide criteria for how to make tough decisions such as these.

Bringing the Vision to Life

Once we had identified our compelling vision for the future, we felt energized and ready to identify three or four strategic priorities it would take to bring this vision to life. The information we'd gotten from our second environmental scan was crucial to this step, helping us to consider the views of internal and external stakeholders and confirm key trends.

A strategic priority is another term for a big idea—often called a major objective, an organizing principle, or a Big Hairy Audacious Goal (BHAG). Whatever the name, the trick is to establish the major priorities necessary to achieve the vision. If a plan has too many priorities, then each one is no longer significant. It becomes a list, not a plan.

We knew that a sound vision would have only three or four big ideas at its core, and it was important to tease these out. Most of our previous strategic plans had five or six key priorities, which were too difficult to juggle.

"Our early plans were divided to ensure that everyone received an equal amount of attention, which really just spread the idea that no one thing was our focus," observed David Page, SDZG's corporate director of finance. "The plans usually had sections for facilities, conservation, new business, animal care, and then one or two specific issues of immediate concern. These plans were separated from the day-to-day work of the organization and never became integrated with our financial plan."

Focusing on too many things meant that we weren't focusing at all. And while having lots of options was a tempting way to get consensus across our planning team, we knew a scattered plan would never lead us to the amazing places we could go.

Narrowing Our Priorities

It was challenging for SDZG to agree on a small number of priorities. To develop a more streamlined list, our board members and executive staff gathered for a daylong workshop to examine the priorities and trade-offs.

- **We brainstormed key priorities.** We explored what we needed to achieve this vision of ending extinction. The group generated a lot of ideas before paring them down to a shorter list of favorites.

- **We ensured that the potential priorities were based on facts, not just opinions.** In previous strategic planning sessions, people would inevitably make statements that they believed to be true. For example, someone might say, "People want to ride their bikes around the Safari Park." This statement might be based on guest feedback, or research about visitor behavior . . . or it might be just an opinion. With this in mind, the executive staff and board members separated into smaller groups to pinpoint what these ideas would look like as organizational priorities—but each small group was asked to identify a trend, fact, or statement from the environmental scan that related to these ideas. This helped rule out ideas that had no supporting information, without making anyone feel criticized.

- **We were careful not to lose anything on the cutting-room floor.** Only three or four "big ideas" could become strategic priorities that fully encompassed the extraordinary effort that would be needed to achieve the new vision. However, even though the executive staff and board didn't select everything as a strategic priority, they captured all the comments and ideas from this phase because each would have a role in the final plans. The group ended the workshop by agreeing to pass the day's ideas on to a strategic-planning steering group for further analysis.

As the team members brainstormed priorities, they also examined the trade-offs, asking the hard question, "What would we give up if we chose this priority over another one?" Every idea that was discussed would move SDZG forward, but not all ideas could be major strategic priorities.

In addition to identifying how each priority would grow the impact of our organization, our executive staff and board members considered how specific ideas would hold us back. They asked: "What would we have to stop doing if this became an overarching strategic priority?" Everyone shifted uncomfortably in their seats as they pondered the question that no one wanted to answer. Every choice meant that SDZG would do more of one thing and less of something else. Which choices would move us toward our vision?

Most of the ideas were rejected because they fell into one of the following categories:

- **Too specific:** We knew that our strategic priorities (in essence, what we chose to do) had to be broad enough to contain several strategies (how we would do it). If the priorities were too specific, SDZG would need dozens of them to achieve our audacious vision. For example, the executive staff and board members discarded the following idea: "Collaborate with others who can sustain our conservation momentum." This idea was vital to vision success, but it ended up becoming a strategy rather than a strategic priority because it explained only one way we would move forward toward fighting extinction. It couldn't encompass all the conservation changes needed to achieve our vision.

- **Too nebulous:** We also did not want strategic priorities that were too vague. These were usually feel-good ideas that sparked excitement but didn't lend themselves to specific strategies for change. They were great for press releases or messaging, so they were cataloged for later use, but they couldn't be labeled as overarching priorities. For example, the team vetoed the idea "Be the best conservation organization in the world" because it wasn't clear. What would make SDZG "the best"? And even if we could define it, how would being "the best" help SDZG work with collaborators to facilitate leading the fight to end extinction?

- **Too little change**: We knew we had a big vision, so we rejected priorities that would represent merely incremental change. Some people suggested priorities that required small steps because they worried that we would lose the progress we'd already made or feared that the plan wasn't achievable. For example, one idea was to "maintain our current programs." But anything that started with "maintain" or "continue" was going to lead us to incremental change, at best. To reach our goal of ending extinction, SDZG had to move outside our comfort zone. The team also recognized that we couldn't maintain all our previous priorities if we wanted to move toward something new—it simply wouldn't be possible!

- **Outside our niche:** It was one thing to recognize where we were going and to set a plan to get there. It was another thing to propose an area in which we had no traction. This was the problem we had during The Lynx years, when we wanted to become a conservation organization but research told us it was out of our grasp within the coming decade. As the executive staff and board worked on the priorities of The Call, they once again weighed priorities outside our niche, including habitat preservation. Ultimately, they decided that while this was a crucial part of saving species, it was not in our wheelhouse. The trade-off to excel at habitat preservation wasn't worth the investment we'd have to make, and it didn't support our plan to work with other conservation organizations. Plus, many of our collaborators already had perfected this niche. Our vision required that we stay focused on saving species and work with other organizations to help ensure their habitat was protected.

- **A core function**: Our strategic priorities needed to encompass a lot— they would serve as the overarching ideas under which all effort toward our vision must fit—but they couldn't include every single thing we would do. We couldn't make priorities out of basic functions like human resources, marketing, finance, administration, and construction. Our new vision would require all departments to participate, but it did not call out one department more than the others. Similarly, while our core values were each integral to bringing the vision to life, they did not individually qualify as a strategic priority. For example, "animal welfare" has always been important to SDZG and always will be. It couldn't be singled out as a strategic priority, though—it is too tightly woven into the fabric of our organization's culture.

- **A result, not a priority**: This was one of the most common issues we faced as we developed our strategic priorities. Many team members wanted to keep their eyes glued to a specific metric so that those results remained top of mind. For example, the executive staff and board knew that financial sustainability would be key to the success of The Call. If we could not remain financially sound, we would not be able to save species. Because of this, the team questioned whether financial success would need to become a strategic priority. We soon realized, however, that although financial sustainability was one of the most crucial ways we would measure success, it wasn't an umbrella for a set of strategies toward leading the fight against extinction. So we talked about the things we would need to do differently to achieve financial sustainability, such as building capacity or making the most of our limited resources. We wrestled with this same issue as we pondered fundraising, employee satisfaction, and other measures. Making these important considerations metrics of success, rather than strategic priorities, would allow us to achieve more in the long run—and provide a way to measure progress toward our vision.

Steering in a New Direction

After the retreat, our board chair at the time, Rick Gulley, worked with Doug Myers to identify a team of four executive staff and four board members—called The Call Steering Group—who could take the concepts and work them into a draft plan. The Vision, Innovation, and Strategy (VIS) team organized this group, keeping the members on task and providing insight on strategic planning best practices. In these meetings, the Steering Group expanded on the ideas raised by the board and staff by vetting the proposed priorities and determining which ones were feasible.

To lead the fight against extinction, the Steering Group realized we would need to become an organization capable of facilitating well-rounded conservation solutions. With this in mind, we would have to dedicate a key portion of

About Strategic Priorities

- Strategic priorities are the "big ideas" that make up the skeleton of your strategic plan.
- Strategic priorities should not be altered throughout the strategic plan's lifetime (likely to be three to five years) unless something drastically changes in the organization's internal or external environment. (Note that it may take three or four strategic plans to achieve your vision. For SDZG, we had three phases of The Lynx strategic plan before we achieved our vision.)
- In addition to identifying how your organization could grow with the selection of each priority, ask, "What would we have to stop doing if this became an overarching strategic priority?"

SDZG's plan to building capacity and maximizing resources. Our organization needed to focus on building capacity internally to provide deeper bench strength—in other words, we needed a plan for helping to expand the skill sets of the board, staff, and volunteers. The Steering Group also understood that we required a more scientific approach to selecting critical collaborators who would increase our conservation reach.

The Call was meant to help save species from extinction, but the group realized that obviously one organization could not save all endangered species simultaneously or immediately. SDZG needed to focus on the species for which we could do the most.

As the Steering Group thought about the implications of these changes, they got more excited. In these meetings, they asked, "What will we be able to achieve for species conservation when we choose our battles, lead the charge, and sustain our momentum? What are the possibilities if we abandon the idea that we can do it alone—and truly focus on recruiting like-minded partners to join us in our cause?"

The Steering Group eventually came up with three strategic priorities for The Call:

- **UNITE, internally and externally, with a laser focus on our cause**
  Focus on stemming the tide of species extinction by rallying our internal stakeholders around our vision and building a mighty league of external collaborators.

- **FIGHT against extinction of animal and plant species**
  Fight extinction with an integrated conservation approach that includes both the species in our care as well as animals and plants in the wild.

- **IGNITE a life-changing passion for wildlife**
  Awaken a global audience to take personal responsibility for the future of wildlife.

These three priorities served as a framework for the rest of The Call. The phrase "UNITE, FIGHT, IGNITE" was also easy to remember as the plan moved forward, rallying staff, board members, volunteers, and partners toward our call to end extinction.

OUTLINING OUR STRATEGIES

"Vision is a destination—a fixed point to which we focus all effort.
Strategy is a route—an adaptable path to get us where we want to go."
Simon Sinek, author and speaker

In addition to determining our strategic priorities (or "big ideas"), The Call Steering Group was also responsible for identifying the strategies that would provide focus within the "UNITE, FIGHT, IGNITE" framework. These strategies would identify *how* San Diego Zoo Global would concentrate on the strategic priorities.

The group's first draft of the strategies came together relatively easily. The material from the environmental scans had told us what needed to be done as well as what our organization was best suited to do. The information we received from the board and executive staff's strategic planning workshop helped to fill in the gaps.

It seemed to The Call Steering Group that the public supported the idea of conservation, but people ignored the plight of wildlife in their everyday lives. The group felt that we would have to do something monumental to get the public to adopt this cause. Animal and plant conservation was competing with dozens of other causes, as well as with the demands of people's personal issues. SDZG couldn't just share the facts of conservation and expect that people would drop everything to save rhinos in Africa or lemurs in Madagascar. Besides, the public probably wouldn't even understand what needed to be done to save wildlife. It had taken SDZG many years to see the big picture—how could we expect the general public to understand the nuances involved in saving entire species of plants and animals?

To spur the public to take conservation action, the Steering Group knew that we needed to come up with strategies and creative methods that would ignite a passion in everyone, including scientists, government officials, guests, and website visitors. This challenge would ultimately help us prioritize and focus our work: we would use scientific methods, animal husbandry solutions, and anything else in our arsenal to lead the charge. We would also collaborate with others who could keep these conservation efforts in place for as long as species were in need.

A Barrage of Bad Ideas

Members of the Steering Group began to see The Call as a fight—a genuine battle against time at a critical juncture in the history of the world. More and more species of animals and plants were headed for extinction, which would require SDZG to awaken a global audience to take personal responsibility for the future of wildlife. As the group's enthusiasm for this approach grew, the language in the strategic plan took on a harsh new urgency. The group talked of battle plans and ammunition and waging war against complacency.

As the draft came together, the Steering Group was excited to share it with staff. Two employee groups reviewed the draft: the executive staff as well as a group called the New Perspectives Strategic Planning Team, which comprised staff members from many departments. To the surprise of the Steering Group, these staff groups did *not* feel inspired by the war analogies. To them, the war terminology felt off-message. They believed that the work to save species was about focus, leadership, and momentum—not the blazing barrage of bullets that the first draft of The Call brought to mind.

The Steering Group took these comments to heart and went back to the drawing board. The resulting strategies weren't based on an analogy but instead showed how we would genuinely achieve our vision. The final strategies are listed below.

Strategies to UNITE

1. **Build Capacity**

   Focus internally and externally on organizational capacity building: select critical collaborators whose strengths increase our reach and boost the bench strength of our staff, board, and volunteers.

2. **Maximize Our Resources**

   Ensure that we have the financial capacity and fiscal responsibility to become the most effective wildlife conservation organization in the world . . . both now and in the future.

Strategies to FIGHT

1. **Pick Our Battles**

   As much as we want to, we can't save every species, and we can't do it alone. We will prioritize and focus our work on the species that are the best fit for our niche.

2. **Lead the Charge**

   Enhance our emphasis on full-spectrum conservation, applying leading-edge scientific methods and husbandry solutions to our priority species.

3. **Sustain the Momentum**

   Collaborate with others who can maintain our conservation efforts as long as necessary.

Strategies to IGNITE

1. **Ignite Passion**

   Spark an obsession for saving wildlife.

2. **Recruit Champions**

   Use grand gestures and unique methods to attract advocates to our cause.

3. **Inspire Personal Responsibility**

   Provide people with a new way of life—specific individual actions that we each must take to make a change in the wildlife conservation landscape.

Adding these strategies to The Call completed the strategic plan overview that would provide a roadmap for SDZG over the next three to five years. "These strategies speak to the difficult choices that need to be made as we move toward our vision," said Robin Keith, associate director of VIS, who participated in facilitating the Steering Group's work. "It was very rewarding to see the strategies take shape and gain acceptance."

Board member Javade Chauhdri, a member of the Steering Group, agreed: "I see many nonprofits that are initially successful, but then they've 'lost the plot' because they are unable to adapt. I'm proud of our willingness to evolve for the future of wildlife." Rick Gulley, also a member of both the board and the Steering Group, put it this way: "These strategies represent a conscious decision on our part. We have a responsibility to do more because of our scope and size and the benefits that have been given to us. We've chosen a higher path."

"For me, the excitement about The Call started to build after we agreed on the strategies. I began to see how we could actually achieve our vision." Robin added.

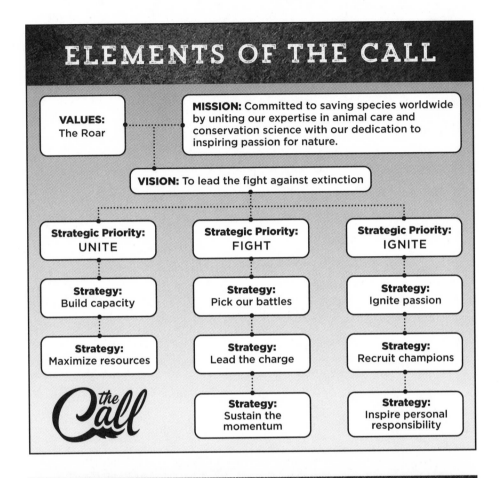

ELEMENTS OF THE CALL

VALUES:
The Roar

MISSION: Committed to saving species worldwide by uniting our expertise in animal care and conservation science with our dedication to inspiring passion for nature.

VISION: To lead the fight against extinction

Strategic Priority:
UNITE

Strategic Priority:
FIGHT

Strategic Priority:
IGNITE

Strategy:
Build capacity

Strategy:
Pick our battles

Strategy:
Ignite passion

Strategy:
Maximize resources

Strategy:
Lead the charge

Strategy:
Recruit champions

Strategy:
Sustain the momentum

Strategy:
Inspire personal responsibility

the Call

About Strategies

- Strategies explain how your strategic priorities will play out.
- Strategies should last for as long as your strategic priorities are in place—usually three to five years.
- Strategies provide the high-level areas of emphasis for each of your strategic priorities. If you "add up" the strategies, they should encompass the major steps needed to realize your vision.

LAUNCHING
THE CALL

ASSEMBLING A NEW BREED
OF STRATEGIC PLAN

"If you can't describe your strategy in 20 minutes, simply and in plain
language, you haven't got a plan. 'But,' people may say, 'I've got a
complex strategy. It can't be reduced to a page.' That's nonsense. That's
not a complex strategy. It's a complex thought about the strategy."
Lawrence Bossidy, author and business leader

Over many months, San Diego Zoo Global had completed all the basic
steps toward crafting The Call: assessing our environment, updating
our mission statement, identifying our core values, and creating an energizing
vision. In addition, our team had outlined the strategic priorities and the strategies that would be necessary to bring the vision to life.

Although we had identified the essential elements of The Call, we had
also learned the value of distilling our concepts, wordsmithing key elements,
and branding our plan. This marked one of the key differences from our previous, lackluster strategic plans: our devotion to refining the strategies of SDZG
down to their essence. On the surface, this sounds like a personal preference
for a shorter plan over a longer one—but it actually represented many hours of

often-frustrating discussion about what each part of the plan actually meant to ensure that all key players understood and endorsed The Call.

That understanding allowed the plan to be:

- **Pared down to a few short elements,** which could then serve as a type of shorthand for those who knew all the actions, strategies, and metrics that underpinned the plan.
- **Communicated to all those who would implement it** in a way that was both meaningful and memorable.
- **A nonstarter for old arguments** that could now be put to bed.
- **A decision-making guide** that empowered employees at all levels of the organization to understand the trade-offs between one course of action and another in relation to The Call.

This last point was truly crucial, and it affected even our collaborative efforts. For example, SDZG was considering a partnership with another wildlife association. Many elements of the collaboration looked positive; there were several ways in which both entities could extend each other's conservation reach. We shared our strategic plan for the future along with a few key projects. In one meeting, we asked the association if working on those key projects together would fit within their own strategic plan. "It will be fine," the association's CEO replied. "Fortunately, our strategic plan is loose enough that anything can fit under it."

The team from SDZG was stunned into silence. After all our work on strategic planning, we knew that if a strategic plan is open to all possible initiatives, it's not a plan that will guide an organization to greatness. Determining an organization's direction takes grit. It forces you to close many doors to be able to open others. Ultimately, we did move forward with the partnership, but we offered to help the association with its next strategic planning effort at no charge.

A Cohesive Strategy That Empowers Workers

Distilled strategies can help achieve organizational outcomes, but they can also be challenging to communicate in a way that empowers staff members to make decisions and still maintain a cohesive strategy. Authors Orit Gadiesh and James L. Gilbert discuss this in their article "Transforming Corner-Office Strategy into Frontline Action."[14] They maintain that the distillation of a company's strategy is important because a brilliant business strategy is of little use unless people understand it well enough to apply it—to both anticipated decisions and unforeseen opportunities.

Strategic principles force trade-offs between competing resource demands, test the strategic soundness of a particular action, and set clear boundaries for employees while granting them freedom to experiment within those constraints. For example, Walmart's strategic principle of "Everyday low prices" clarifies the company's priorities. General Electric's longtime strategic principle "Be number one or number two in every industry in which we compete—or get out" helps the company decide when to say no. And SDZG's vision of "Leading the fight against extinction" serves as our strategic principle, clarifying our role and our goal.

In their article, Gadiesh and Gilbert also talk about the example of Southwest Airlines, whose strategic principle was to "Meet customers' short-haul travel needs at fares competitive with the cost of automobile travel." They attribute much of Southwest's rapid growth to the ability to stay focused on their strategic principle. In 1983, Southwest began offering service to Denver, a high-traffic destination that made sense for the company. However, the airline experienced longer and more consistent delays at the Denver airport than anywhere else. The delays were caused by a variety of factors related to the weather, and Southwest realized the only way to remain in Denver was to increase ticket prices.

To determine the best course of action, the company turned to its strategic principle. They asked, "Would we be able to maintain fares consistent with the cost of car travel?" The answer was clearly no, and Southwest pulled out of Denver within three years. Later, the company returned to Denver when conditions changed.

Wordsmithing Key Elements

At SDZG, we used a strategic planning process that focused on "concepts first, then wordsmithing." There is an inherent push to play with the wording of concepts as they emerge. Many strategic planning team participants like to find their thesaurus and start scrolling for the perfect word choice. Instead, we relied on a strategic facilitator to continually push our group to work through the meaning of the concepts until we were totally comfortable with the trade-offs inherent in each. Our strategic planning team members were frequently frustrated by the facilitator's insistence on avoiding wordsmithing—but once we finally agreed on the concepts, we could let the compelling language emerge.

Unfortunately, the people who have the best handle on the strategic needs of the organization are rarely the same ones who should be wordsmithing the plan. Here's how we navigated this phase:

- **We ensured the plan's wordsmithing was done by as few people as possible**. As we learned, groups do not wordsmith well; they often fall victim to compromise and quibble about word choice. We chose two or three people to bounce ideas off one another.
- **We tapped our best internal wordsmiths for crafting the language of the plan.** Our wordsmiths were not always executives or board members, but they had a talent for translating ideas into clear and compelling language.
- **We included a strategic planning professional in the wordsmithing phase.** Our planners not only knew the intent behind the concepts but also could help us steer clear of language that was either too vague to

guide implementation, too technical to cross all audiences, or too narrowly focused to survive the life of our plan.

- **We made it inspirational but kept the original ideas intact.** During the creative process, our wordsmiths made liberal use of evocative wording and memorable phrases—but they also remained true to the concepts approved by the strategic planning team as well as strategic planning best practices.

- **We reduced the signal-to-noise ratio.** During the strategic planning team's conceptual phase, we agreed on concepts that had many more words than necessary. Condensing these down to their essence helped us make the strategic plan memorable and excite others to join our cause.

- **We structured the feedback**. Once the wording was fine-tuned, we provided a short window of time for our strategic planning team to comment on the drafts and to request another round with the wordsmiths if needed. Ultimately, the language had to resonate strongly with the planning team, since they would have a pivotal role in making the plan a success. We noticed there was a tendency at this point for the strategic planning team members to want to throw new ideas into the mix, particularly when we asked for open-ended feedback on the wordsmiths' draft. We forestalled this by providing a rubric that asked strategic planning team members to respond to the following questions about the draft: Does it convey the intended meaning outlined in the conceptual plan? Is it inspirational? Is it clear? Does it have more words than necessary?

Branding Our Plan

After wordsmithing, we focused on branding. The Call—like its predecessor, The Lynx—has both a name and an identity. Why is this important? At SDZG, we have staff and volunteers stationed around the world, so we need a memorable plan.

During the early years of The Lynx, SDZG wrestled with this concept. Staff and volunteers were bombarded with "priority messages," making it hard to distinguish the most significant from the mundane. Busy workers would clock in for a shift, then scan bulletin boards or newsletters for the pertinent information they needed. These communication hubs overflowed with helpful information. The strategic plan update would be positioned near "Top tips for eating healthy," safety reminders, and a list of animal births. We wanted the staff and volunteers to understand the strategic plan and to put it into action, but with thousands of workers and volunteers—many of them unfamiliar with strategic planning language—The Lynx got lost in the fray. We used every communication method at our disposal, but we still had trouble gaining traction.

Branding our plan—giving it a name and a visual identity—allowed us to sum up the meaning of the plan in a few succinct words. For The Lynx, a logo depicting the cat it was named for was used throughout the life of the vision. It helped confirm that the plan was still going strong.

The new plan could not be represented by a single species, though. The idea of leading the fight against extinction was so lofty that we needed a powerful name and image. Throughout the planning process, we kept coming back to the idea that the plan must be strong enough to wake people up. We needed a "wake-up call" to rouse them to take notice of the plight of wildlife. We needed a "call to action" to get people to take a stand for animals and plants. We needed to compel people to "hear the call" that would ignite a life-changing passion for wildlife.

Soon, we realized that the name "The Call" best characterized the sense of urgency at the core of our new strategic plan. For the plan's visual identity, we used a distinctive type treatment as our logo, combined with various animals that were a priority for SDZG.

When we unveiled the name and visual identity of The Call in 2015, the vision immediately resonated with staff, volunteers, and board members. Every time we saw the logo of the plan, it reminded us of our fight to end extinction.

Making It Memorable

With The Call, we came to see that a transformational strategic plan was—at its core—the memorable, distilled expression of shared organizational goals.

SAN DIEGO ZOO GLOBAL STRATEGIC PLAN

CHAPTER

12

THE FIRST 100 DAYS

"It's not what the vision is, it's what the vision does."
Peter Senge, management author and speaker

After the Steering Group finished refining The Call, the next step was to convince the San Diego Zoo Global board of trustees. The Steering Group needed to get the strategic plan approved by the full board and—more than that—to make sure every board member was engaged with the plan.

All the Steering Group members took a role in presenting the plan to the board for approval, focusing on the facts that had led to each section of the plan and explaining why each choice had been made. The trustees were won over by the logic of the plan, the need for change, and the audacious dream of ending extinction. They adopted The Call unanimously.

The next step was to get our nearly 6,000 staff members and volunteers to understand the plan and endorse it. We began the launch by sharing the plan—and the process that had led up to it—with employees via presentations at both the Zoo and the Safari Park. The presenters included our CEO, Doug Myers; executive staff members; and members of the New Perspectives Strategic Planning Team, which represented most of SDZG's departments.

After the presentations at the Zoo and the Safari Park, we celebrated. At SDZG, we don't always celebrate success—once something is complete, we usually move on to the next thing. This time, though, we wanted the staff and volunteers to see that their hard work during The Lynx years and their help with the strategic planning process for The Call had led them to this point—and that SDZG would need all of them on board with The Call.

During the rollout events, groups of staff members were invited to pose next to life-sized photos of rhinos, penguins, and cheetahs. They were encouraged to write a pledge on a chalkboard about how they would bring The Call to life and then to take photographs.

The pledges resonated with the staff and volunteers and set the tone from the beginning that everyone would be working together to achieve The Call. Here are just a few of the chalkboard pledges, from employee groups in departments across the organization:

We will ignite guests to care about wildlife.

We will improve nutrition for rhinos.

We will share conservation information with our guests to inspire them.

We will connect communities with conservation.

We will unite to save species.

We will sell merchandise that helps endangered species.

We will release clapper rails into the wild.

We will empower our employees to lead the charge.

We will raise money for endangered species.

We will remove disease as a barrier to conservation.

We will promote science to save species.

We will ignite passion for wildlife in hundreds of students.

We will tell the world . . . one person at a time!

The First 100 Days of Progress

SDZG realized that the first 100 days of internal implementation for The Call would be critical. The staff, board members, and volunteers would all need to see that The Call truly meant that we would *change our actions*, not just communicate differently.

Toward that end, the executive staff identified five key initiatives that could genuinely be achieved in the first 100 days. Although these initiatives represented significant effort (some more than others), they were "quick wins" because they provided highly visible signs of organizational change. Working on these five initiatives also helped the executive staff to bond around The Call during the critical period of early adoption.

In the first 100 days, we focused on the following five key initiatives:

- Bring the Center for Plant Conservation to San Diego for a new kind of collaboration that immediately enabled us to expand our conservation reach in the botanical community.
- Make progress toward reducing wildlife trafficking.
- Work to build a rhino conservation center where scientific solutions to prevent rhino species extinction could be incubated and implemented.
- Set the stage for a collaborative group of local agencies and organizations to agree that "no native species will go extinct in San Diego County on our watch."
- Develop a tool to help staff members evaluate their own workload and say no to projects or programs that were not aligned with The Call.

The First 100 Days of Engagement

To engage everyone on staff, SDZG used a number of methods to communicate, ensuring the plan would be memorable. We took every opportunity to make the plan noteworthy during the launch period.

For instance, our management team committed to communicating about

The Call to some internal audience every single day for the first 100 days. Early on, we communicated about the plan's components. Over time, we included elements of progress toward the five key initiatives to demonstrate that we were beginning in earnest.

SDZG used every internal communications vehicle available, including employee newsletters, daily bulletins, board updates, volunteer announcements, presentations for supervisors, discussions at executive staff meetings, town hall meetings with our CEO, and notices posted in various locations.

In addition to traditional methods, we communicated in creative ways. For example, the volunteer crew posted facts about The Call in their bathrooms. Each bathroom stall was devoted to one of the strategic priorities— UNITE, FIGHT, or IGNITE—and new information was added every week.

We also created as many take-home opportunities as possible, making the chalkboard pledges and photo sessions available at other presentations, departmental gatherings, and events. We distributed pocket-sized versions of The Call, dubbed "Calling Cards," to staff, volunteers, and board members too. They listed every element of The Call—the mission, vision, values, strategic priorities, and strategies—but without the explanatory text. And we handed out phone wallets highlighting The Call's logo along with the Calling Cards. The phone wallets, which attached to the back of staff members' and volunteers' cell phones, could be used for anything: credit cards, employee ID cards, or to hold a Calling Card.

It's All Connected

Within the first 100 days of implementation, our department heads worked to connect their staff responsibilities to The Call. Adoption started at the top. Dwight Scott, the San Diego Zoo director, had served on The Call Steering Committee, so he was dedicated to ensuring that his staff members were on board. He said, "I tell our employees, 'If we're going to lead the fight against extinction, how can we make sure that our guests are as inspired and connected as possible? What can we do differently to make the most impact? How can we ensure that our guests are aware that the animals here are not only healthy but that they also serve as ambassadors for endangered members of their species in the wild?'"

Dwight's enthusiasm was contagious and inspired Michelle Pierce, the director of retail operations at the Zoo, to get the ball rolling. Michelle's department was a huge business unit responsible for merchandise sales as well as food service. "The Call is an effective strategic plan that all employees can rally behind, knowing that their work contribution has higher meaning," Michelle pointed out. "Retail is the largest department of frontline employees, and The Call gives us a blueprint to teach our staff about where we are headed. It allows us to improve our quality of guest service, better engage employees, and increase sales. All this supports our efforts to end extinction. Employees who have been trained now understand their daily efforts have meaning far beyond selling a T-shirt or pouring a soft drink: they have personal responsibility for saving species. We've seen evidence of The Call's effectiveness range from increased employee survey scores and guest-satisfaction survey scores to unprecedented sales records."

Michelle inspired her staff leaders to develop training programs that would pull it all together. One of her managers, Melinda Truett, was assigned to renovate the retail training program. "The training program had been around for so long that people couldn't recall when it had been put in place. I created a draft of a new program and brought it to Michelle Pierce for review," said Melinda. "She challenged me to see The Call launch presentation and then to revamp my training program with this in mind. As I watched The Call roll out, a light went on in my head."

Melinda knew that the retail workers admired the veterinarians, keepers, and scientists because they worked directly with wildlife. So her new training program focused on helping the retail employees see themselves as an integral part of SDZG's conservation team as well. She wanted them to be engaged with their work and with the guests. Her theory was that the investment would pay off in increased employee satisfaction, increased guest satisfaction, and—hopefully—increased sales.

Melinda set up a system to report animal and conservation news to the retail workers and explained that the money they took in funded many of these efforts. She allowed them to take short breaks while on the clock (she called it "wild time") to visit their favorite Zoo animals, and then she encouraged the staff members to share their experiences with each other.

Melinda's new training program not only taught the retail staff how to sell products, it also helped them engage with Zoo guests. In every sales transaction, there are a few seconds of downtime while the soft drink cup is filled or the cash register approves a credit card. Melinda asked her staff to use that time to ask each visitor a simple, observant question. For example, if a guest's child was holding a plush polar bear, the salesperson might ask if the family had been to see the polar bears yet. "Much of it sounds simple," Melinda said, "but in the past, our retail team had been told that they were here to make money. Period. They weren't connected to the bigger picture. They weren't connecting with the guests."

Melinda's program encouraged the frontline staff members to write up their exceptional guest encounters and submit them to a departmental newsletter. Every issue was packed with these inspirational stories, which encouraged other employees to raise the bar. "One of the early examples that struck me was from a woman who worked in a snack stand," Melinda recalled. "She was heading out of the stand to take a break when a guest came up and asked her where the Reptile House was. She walked the guest to the lizards, saying, 'Here are the reptiles. Let me show you my favorites.' She makes fries and cheeseburgers when she's on the clock. She did this on her own time."

Melinda's retail training program became hugely successful, and it was soon being measured and considered for other business units as well. "What I love about The Call," Melinda said, "is that it focuses on the big picture. In the past, the revenue-generating departments—such as retail—were only motivated to bring in money. If you worked behind a cash register, that was your focus. Now, with The Call, our staff members can say, 'I'm not just here to process financial transactions. I'm here to help our guests learn to love animals as much as I do.' It's an enormous paradigm shift. Our retail workers see that they're encouraged to engage with guests now. What it has done for morale is huge, and it has allowed us to connect with and enjoy the guests. I told my staff, 'Your cheeks should hurt at the end of the day from smiling and talking. Enjoy yourselves!' I've worked for a lot of other companies where the bottom line was sales, rather than caring and connection. It's empowering and addictive!"

Building Buy-In, Group by Group

After launching The Call, SDZG set up a recurring communications plan to ensure that our bold vision to end extinction remained top of mind. We customized this plan to meet the needs of every group.

Executives

- We dedicated one executive staff meeting every month to thoroughly examining our strategic plan successes and roadblocks.
- Each executive created a strategic plan for his or her own business unit, using The Call as a guide.
- We aligned the annual organizational goals with The Call, using the plan's eight strategies as categories that would funnel down to individual employee goals.

Engagement Tool

SDZG circulated the following information about why we were pursuing The Call to help staff and volunteers understand the reasons for taking this new direction:

San Diego Zoo Global represents nearly a century of work on behalf of wildlife, but the state of wildlife is now at a critical juncture. San Diego Zoo Global is uniquely positioned to lead the fight against wildlife extinction.

- **Why us? Why now?** San Diego Zoo Global is financially strong and operates two world-renowned parks as well as wildlife conservation efforts. So, why choose such an audacious vision? Because species are disappearing faster than ever and stemming the tide of extinction will take enormous creativity, resources, and focus. Despite our decades-long commitment to conservation, animal and plant species continue to vanish at record speeds.

- **We are at a crossroads.** We could choose to continue on our current path. San Diego Zoo Global has a great track record of operational excellence and wildlife conservation results. But our research shows that we are the best organization to serve as a catalyst among our peers and partners by taking on a new role in the global community. Our external review shows there is hope for saving species on a grand scale in the coming decade, but not without a transformational shift in our priorities and a sea change in our approach.

- **We must earn a leadership role.** Delivering on our vision won't be easy. It will require a plan that challenges the status quo, one that forces us to admit that we can no longer continue along our current trajectory. Leading this fight against extinction can only be earned through sustained focus, an unflinching look at our organization, and a willingness to take bold steps to adapt.

- **We can't succeed alone.** Achieving our vision will be impossible without key collaboration with others who have complementary areas of expertise. San Diego Zoo Global will have to conduct itself in a highly professional, flexible, and innovative manner. We will have to seize the public's attention, energize people, and appeal to the media . . . because these practices will become the engines of our message and its execution.

- **We need to develop ways to radically slow the rate of species decline.** If we truly want to lead the fight against extinction, we need to recognize both the magnitude and timeline of what will be required and then develop collaborative strategies in many fields to address this emergency.

- **We are ready for the challenge.** We are eager to get started on the road to our new vision. This will be a long, tough, complicated challenge that will require a multifaceted approach to achieve transformational results. At San Diego Zoo Global, though, we aren't going to settle for anything less.

Managers

- We made an annual presentation about The Call to all supervisors. It included results of various initiatives along with tools that managers could use in their own departments.
- Executives presented updates on their progress at bimonthly managers' meetings.
- We offered updated presentations about The Call throughout the year to departments that requested one.

Staff and volunteers

- CEO Doug Myers held an annual "all-hands meeting" that included every employee and volunteer, focusing his presentation on The Call. Having our CEO use the plan's terminology and metrics in his presentation inspired the entire team.
- We offered quarterly forums for all staff. These forums allowed for presentations on key initiatives—such as conservation projects, new alliances, or systems—as well as an opportunity for the staff to ask Doug questions.
- We shared progress on The Call in employee and volunteer newsletters and daily bulletins.
- We put up posters featuring different elements of The Call on every level of the Zoo's employee parking structure.
- We gave a pocket-sized version of The Call to every employee, volunteer, and intern.

Board members

- We created a beautiful, high-end brochure of The Call. The brochure was made for external audiences, but it also helped board members to share the plan with colleagues and potential donors.

- Board members aligned their own annual goals with The Call and used the plan to develop our CEO's goals as well. This ensured that every board meeting would include a discussion of some element of the plan.
- The annual budget not only included financial projections that were aligned with The Call, but also a narrative linking the metrics of The Call to the proposed budget.

Communicating the plan to different groups in various ways created much-needed buy-in—ultimately helping ensure the success of the plan and our grand vision. Mark Stuart, SDZG's chief development and membership officer, knows a lot about the value of a bold vision. He said, "I'm a preacher's kid, and my father had a passage hanging in the office, paraphrased from the Book of Proverbs that said, 'Without vision, the people shall perish. With great vision, the people shall flourish.' SDZG has a grand vision, and by focusing on our grand vision, not only will we flourish, but our activities will succeed as well. Ask anyone what our vision is: they can recite it proudly. By focusing on it, we know that we can move forward boldly and The Call will guide our efforts."

UNITING AROUND
A COMMON CAUSE

"This plan is a wake-up call: to unite people to our cause, to fight against extinction, and to ignite a life-changing passion for wildlife."
The Call Strategic Plan

After The Call was launched, it came to life as more of a movement than a framework. Everyone—frontline staff, volunteers, executives, board members—embraced it, remembered it, and lived it.

Michael Mace, director of animal collections and strategy, noted the immediate internal impact: "In longstanding organizations such as ours, it's difficult to change the culture of 3,000 employees overnight. The reason that The Call is so compelling for us is because every employee feels empowered to help lead the fight to end extinction."

Katie Cox, a San Diego Zoo Global human resources benefits specialist, saw The Call's impact within the first six months. "As we were conducting exit interviews with interns, we asked them what they found most rewarding about working here, and—unaided—they cited The Call. These were entry-level internships in retail, buildings and grounds, and camp aide positions.

They loved it here because they understood how they fit into the fight against extinction. One young staffer commented, 'Every time I sold something, I knew it was helping conservation. It made my job exciting.'" Katie concluded, "Everyone talks about The Call. It's part of our everyday language. We're now an organization that has everyone working toward the same goal."

In addition to existing employees, The Call appealed to potential job candidates. Dr. Don Janssen, SDZG's retired corporate director of animal health, recalled a time he needed to hire a nutritionist soon after the launch of The Call. "I sent potential candidates a job description as well as a copy of The Call. By the next day, I had received 12 responses that specifically referenced The Call. It was obvious that potential employees saw it as something they wanted to be associated with."

Judy Kinsell, director of corporate and foundation relations, agreed: "Our mission and vision have been infused with energy and now carry a sense of urgency. I can't remember ever sending a strategic plan to a donor in the past unless it was required by a foundation as an attachment. Today, I proudly send The Call to conservation donors because I want them to know how fully committed we are and that we will live up to our bold and ambitious mission and vision. The Call ensures that their investments in conservation are well placed in us."

The initial acceptance helped in many ways, particularly by enabling us to "UNITE." By being united, we could focus on building capacity and maximizing resources necessary to form the foundation for a new kind of organization.

A Mighty League of Collaborators

Throughout our history, SDZG has always worked to engage collaborators. The key difference with The Call was that we were now focused on our role as facilitators of conservation action. This happened internally as well as externally. Internally, the need for integration was reflected in our new mission statement, which emphasized that our efforts to save species would be achieved by uniting our expertise across SDZG. It wasn't enough to conduct good science; now that we had a long-term view of conservation, we needed to align all our efforts with it.

With The Call, our conservation efforts around the globe expanded to include not only our scientists but also our public relations professionals, educators, and many others. We sought to join forces with external partners by prioritizing those species for which we could provide the most benefit. The Call also ushered in a shift in the way we viewed collaboration. Sometimes organizations that partner together are subtly (or not so subtly) competitive, concerned that they are vying for the same donor dollars, grant funding, patron attendance, and so on. The Call was based on the premise that we would "lead the fight," meaning that we would facilitate the collective work of our many partners to ensure that we achieved more together. We no longer saw ourselves as competing with other conservation organizations; instead, SDZG concentrated on what was needed to solve species' conservation issues holistically and then sought to fill the gaps between our own work and that of others.

Among the most striking examples of our commitment to collaboration is SDZG's work with the Center for Plant Conservation (CPC)—a nonprofit network of 40 botanical institutions whose mission is to conserve and restore the rare native plants of the United States. At SDZG, we realized that we needed to step up our game in terms of saving plant species. Recognizing that The Call required partnership and a facilitative approach, we sought to create a new kind of collaboration with the CPC.

The process was challenging. "We wanted to bring the CPC to San Diego and work with the organization as collaborators while providing staff positions at SDZG to the CPC leaders," recalled Dr. Bob Wiese, chief life sciences officer. "This required a huge leap of faith." SDZG's horticulture staff was already working on behalf of plants, but bringing the CPC on board would

About Alignment and Excitement

- In a nonprofit organization or association, staff and volunteers are both your most ardent fans and your harshest critics. They care deeply about your cause and feel personally invested in delivering on the mission. There is a huge value—often underestimated—in getting them excited and involved with your strategic plan.

- Your staff and volunteers will not be satisfied with meager results. To get them on board, you must continually demonstrate the ways in which the organization's results relate to the strategic plan. Don't expect people to make these connections on their own.

- Your strategic plan must be aligned with your financial plan to accomplish truly transformative change. Many strong plans fail when they rely on a desired windfall to fund the plan in its entirety. Even if the windfall arrives, you must continually show your staff and volunteers that you are committed to allocating the current resources in alignment with your plan. Nothing showcases your dedication more than the way you allocate the limited resources of your organization.

- To roll out a strong strategic plan, it's critical to collaborate internally and agree on how you will look differently at funding mechanisms. You'll want to ensure that you can inspire new funding sources but also that you can make the hard choices that will allow you to prioritize the needs of your strategic plan.

allow the organization to contribute so much more to the field of plant conservation. Under the new partnership, SDZG would be able to help save endangered plants by bringing them into cultivation or seed banks, backed up by research, applied conservation, and technological innovation. "To make this work, our CEO, Doug, had to use all available open positions for the year to integrate CPC staff members. Many other departments were asking for additional resources or new positions, but Doug stuck to his guns and supported The Call," said Bob. By the end of The Call's first 100 days, the CPC was on board, and its executive director was packing his bags for a move to San Diego.

Peter Gilson, an educator/guide at the San Diego Zoo, has also seen the collaboration firsthand. "One of the greatest impacts of The Call I have personally experienced is increased internal collaboration, driven by an improved focus on our collective goal of saving species," Peter said. "Although our scientists are leaders in their respective fields, some of our conservation goals had remained unrealized in the past because we were spread too thin to address the human dimension of conservation for some species. The Call created opportunities for some of us in other departments to help out."

Although SDZG was experienced at helping endangered wildlife, we also needed to partner with indigenous people on conservation issues and explore how they could make lifestyle changes that would save wildlife without sacrificing their livelihoods. Peter explained that the increased internal collaboration advocated by The Call allowed him to conduct teacher workshops and lead educational programs for students in critical conservation areas like rural Mexico and on remote Fijian islands. "These contributions to our global conservation work have given me a greater sense of purpose in fulfilling our mission," Peter said. "Whether here at home or across the world, The Call has made it easy for me to see how my daily work directly relates to our fight to end extinction."

Another educator/guide, Colleen Bowman, said, "One of the many reasons I love working for the San Diego Zoo is the passion and excitement that everyone dedicates to our common goal of wildlife conservation." Colleen works to end extinction by sharing SDZG's conservation efforts with guests through interactive presentations and outreach programming. One species she talks about is the critically endangered saiga antelope, known for its unusual snout, which is an adaptation for living in a dry, cold, and dusty environment. SDZG has partnered with the Saiga Conservation Alliance on an education initiative, working to teach children in the saiga's range— Mongolia, Russia, and Uzbekistan—about the animal that shares their home. "Not only has this alliance united us with a cause on the other side of the world," explained Colleen, "but it has also ignited a passion in children for an important part of their ecosystem and culture."

CHANGING OUR BATTLE PLANS

*"San Diego Zoo Global, through its strategic plan, is committed
to saving endangered animals and plants throughout the world with
the help of many organizations. We recognize the importance of
preserving our planet through animals and plants and educating the
community on how they can become partners with us."*
Berit Durler, former SDZG board chair and trustee emeritus

In September 2016, as many as 100 staff, board members, and guests stood in a circle at the San Diego Zoo Safari Park. It was a hot day, but all eyes were on a flaming fire pit where one million dollars' worth of confiscated rhino horns burned. Some of the horns were whole; others had been carved into decorative objects. The pit also contained the powdered remains of horns ground up for falsely touted "medicinal purposes"—a common reason for killing rhinos.

For those watching, the burn seemed symbolic at first—there was a great deal of satisfaction that poachers would not be profiting from the horns of these rhinos. But as we gazed at that fire, the situation suddenly became real for us. The horns in that pit came from white rhinos, black rhinos, and greater one-horned rhinos. It was a sickening, emotional experience for us to watch the horns burn and imagine the illegal slaughter of majestic rhinos in the wild.

A collaboration spearheaded by the US Fish and Wildlife Service, the burn brought much-needed attention to the rhino-poaching crisis. It was the first of its kind in the nation, a joint outreach effort that included many government agencies and made a significant impact on social media and major news outlets, igniting coverage as wide-ranging as an article in the *Los Angeles Times* to a feature on the evening news in Sydney, Australia. It also served as a warning to rhino-horn smugglers that the government was serious about stopping this illegal trade. By focusing on the collaborative role of leading the fight against extinction, we were able to rally our resources around the cause.

The rhino-horn burn was not something we would have done in the past. It was a bold and audacious way to bring light to an important conservation issue, and it was just one of many innovative solutions that we employed after the launch of The Call.

Board member Dr. Linda Lowenstine said, "With The Call, San Diego Zoo Global shifted from a zoo that did conservation to a conservation organization that uses its zoo-derived resources to promote and conduct conservation in a holistic way—at home and in the field. It was one of the most exciting and unifying 'movements' I've seen in any organization." Linda said it energized and empowered employees at all levels of the organization: "From groundskeepers to animal care staff, to scientists and administrators, to the merchandising warehouse and those of us on the board . . . it allowed us to speak with clarity and address urgent matters, such as wildlife trafficking, with one voice and from a position of integrity."

Seeing the Big Picture

For decades, SDZG had been involved in conservation projects for the species in our care at the San Diego Zoo and San Diego Zoo Safari Park, working to help the animals' wild counterparts. But the staff leaders who oversaw these efforts operated, for the most part, in a vacuum from the conservation research being conducted at the San Diego Zoo Institute for Conservation Research. Previous strategic plans brought these groups together, but The Call demanded a more integrated approach.

The Call also helped SDZG veterinarians to see their role in the larger landscape of species conservation. Dr. Beth Bicknese, a senior veterinarian, explained, "As wildlife veterinarians, we apply the medical knowledge we have learned in zoos to entire animal populations when we work on conservation projects in the wild."

For instance, SDZG has learned a lot about overcoming the difficulties of raising baby birds at the Zoo, and this knowledge has been passed on to the conservation work we do in the field. "What we've learned has been applied to help the critically endangered Galápagos mangrove finch in the Galápagos Islands off Ecuador," Beth noted. This husbandry knowledge and medical-management expertise has been used to help other birds such as the San Clemente loggerhead shrike, the Mariana crow, and several species of endangered Hawaiian forest birds.

"The individual animal medicine we learned in the past is helping us maintain critical assurance populations that are preventing extinction in many species," she continued. "To me, The Call exemplifies what the veterinary department does: we work hard to save animals, which saves species either through that particular animal or through the knowledge we gain to help others in that species. Saving animals, and hence populations, is what we do daily."

Picking Our Battles

The Call's "FIGHT" strategic priority compelled us to battle species extinction with an integrated conservation approach that included both the species in our care as well as plants and animals in the wild. The Call also prompted us to develop a new prioritization process to help us choose our conservation battles wisely.

In 2018, we launched the Priority Species Process, a fully integrated, species-based approach to evaluating and selecting conservation projects. The Priority Species Process is a game-changer for SDZG. The process allows us to strategically focus resources on a set of priority species. It also highlights opportunities for cross-departmental partnership and synergy and brings attention to the links between animals in our care in San Diego, lab bench research, and our field efforts around the world.

The process starts with selecting species based on several factors, including conservation need, inter- and intra-organizational collaboration, long-term project goals and commitments, and the best fit within our conservation niche. Next, we create a list of outcomes that must be achieved to ensure species survival. We complete a matrix for each species identified as a priority, based on the Priority Species Process criteria. The matrix captures whether conservation outcomes are being actively addressed—either by SDZG or by a collaborator. Gaps in the matrix—outcomes that are not being addressed by SDZG or our partners—guide the allocation of resources and selection of conservation activities.

For example, desert tortoises were chosen as a priority species for 2018. The full-spectrum analysis showed us that—along with our partners—we were already providing population monitoring and research, biobanking of cells that represented the living population, health and nutrition management, educational outreach, community capacity building, and advocacy for the population of desert tortoises. The analysis also showed that other conservation entities were conducting activities that added to the full-spectrum conservation approach for desert tortoises, such as conducting a threat assessment of the current environment, providing and restoring protected habitat, and writing legislation to protect the species. But there were still gaps in the overall desert tortoise conservation landscape. No conservation entity had yet taken the reins to establish an assurance population—meaning a genetically diverse group of tortoises safeguarded in managed care as an "assurance" in the event that disease or a natural disaster decimated the wild population. There was also no organization with a plan in place to bank gametes (sperm or eggs).

The matrix has provided much-needed information for the desert tortoise and for many other species. By looking at the full spectrum of all these wildlife conservation elements, we are able to work with our partners to address species conservation needs comprehensively and pursue additional collaborators as needed. The matrix provides a set of outcomes by which to measure the impact of our conservation work. Where previous conservation metrics captured only activities (such as the number of species in a breeding program), the new full-spectrum metrics help monitor conservation outcomes as well (for example, genetic management of assurance populations).

"It has really changed the way we look at each conservation issue," said Robin Keith, the SDZG associate director of Vision, Innovation, and Strategy (VIS). "The Priority Species Process tells us which species we can truly help, based on the work done by us or by our partners. It also identifies the gaps so that we can help fill them if they are in our niche or identify collaborators if they are outside our areas of expertise."

WE HAVE IGNITION!

"Big thinking precedes great achievement."
Wilferd Peterson, author and journalist

The "IGNITE" section of The Call sparked an obsession for saving wildlife, attracted advocates to our cause, and inspired personal responsibility. While The Lynx strategic plan series had required continuous, deliberate effort to engage and remind employees of the organization's direction, The Call practically ignited on its own, generating response almost immediately. This "ignition" was crucial for our staff and volunteers, but the greater result came when we shared our passion externally: with guests at the San Diego Zoo and San Diego Zoo Safari Park, visitors to San Diego Zoo Global's websites, and partners throughout the world.

The Call required grand gestures and unique methods to attract advocates to our cause. In particular, our tour guides, who interact with millions of guests each year, were vital to getting the word out, relaying species information and key conservation work that SDZG and our partners are doing around the globe.

"Soon after The Call was launched, I observed one of our bus tour guides describing how using sustainable palm oil helps save tigers and orangutans in

Southeast Asia," recalled Drew Searing, a lead tour operator guide at the Zoo. "The bus driver mentioned that SDZG is a member of the RSPO [Roundtable for Sustainable Palm Oil] and shared their website. When she mentioned a phone app that helps consumers choose products that contain sustainable palm oil, I witnessed two women sitting near me checking their phones. I overheard one say, 'Oh, good, Girl Scout cookies are safe.' The other said, 'Uh-oh, time to switch my shampoo!' Later, when our tour guide pointed out the rainwater collection system at the Australian Outback Queenslander building, a couple sitting in front of me commented, 'We need to start doing that at home!' As I listened, I realized this is proof that all of us here at SDZG are uniting, fighting, and especially igniting our guests into action. This is exactly why I am proud to work here and cannot think of a more rewarding job!"

Lee Rendon, a senior tour operator guide, also noticed the change: "After my tours, which now include information on our many worldwide conservation efforts, I frequently hear positive comments and concerns about helping animals. Many guests have expressed their appreciation for the work SDZG is doing and are interested in how they can also help make a difference in their own lives. I know our tour messages are reaching many people each day, helping to educate and inspire them to make a difference in the world. Our message to end extinction is working . . . one person at a time."

SDZG's volunteers—nearly 3,000 of them—are another invaluable source of information for guests. Art Wells, an information ambassador and interpretive volunteer, noted, "Most people are so wrapped up in their own everyday survival. Part of our job is to slightly expand that view to include helping plant and animal species survive. Without SDZG's vigilance, our future generations would have fewer animal and plant species in their world—people would only be able to see photos of certain species, instead of actual animals or plants. We are trying to awaken and generate a spark in each of our guests so they will help us end extinction."

One of the reasons The Call resonates so well with staff and volunteers is because it is simple and concise. David Foster, development supervisor for SDZG, commented, "To me, The Call is indeed a call to action in all aspects of our lives. It is a pledge for a change in attitude and lifestyle. It leads to a dedication to sustainability and collaboration. We, as employees of SDZG, must lead by example. We must be the change we seek, and The Call is our blueprint to align our personal visions with that of SDZG."

Sunni Robertson, lead educator/guide at the San Diego Zoo, told a story of how she realized the value of The Call. "I was asked to come to my daughter's elementary school assembly to deliver a San Diego Zoo presentation about recycling," Sunni recalled. "We discussed ways the kids can help wildlife by creating less trash." The program addressed many items that were often found in school lunches and explained how these items could hurt animals and the environment. "To help kids take action, we showed them that they could keep squeezable plastic drink pouches out of the landfill by 'upcycling' them through an outside company that would repurpose them for future use."

That night, Sunni picked up her daughter and found 10 plastic drink pouches in her backpack. "As I pulled out one after another, I asked her, 'Where did you get all of these?' She explained that her friends who had drink pouches for lunch that day gave them to her so she could bring them to me so they could be upcycled to help wildlife." Sunni said this continued for weeks. "I was surprised and inspired by how much the assembly and our call to action had moved the students to continuously divert their trash from the landfill. I've always been passionate about my job but this renewed my belief that SDZG can and does have an impact on our community. A school assembly program had certainly ignited a passion in all those schoolchildren to save wildlife, and they took action in the best way they knew how—as evidenced by my growing collection of drink pouches."

The Future of Conservation Learning

Soon after the launch of The Call, we found an opportunity to build capacity, not just within staff but also among our collaborators. The SDZG board of trustees had charged our staff leaders with hosting a symposium to consider the future of conservation learning. Originally, this was intended only for SDZG staff, but The Call urged us to think bigger—to build capacity internally *and* externally. We opened the symposium up to a broader conservation learning community. In October 2015, 200 participants from more than 50 zoos, aquariums, museums, and parks gathered in San Diego for the Future of Informal Conservation Learning Symposium. This event featured keynote presentations from experts in the field and breakout discussions that explored current research, best practices, and innovations in conservation learning theory and practice.

"The symposium taught us a lot about how to bring about human behavior change," said Robin Keith, associate director of Vision, Innovation, and Strategy (VIS). "Human activity is driving species loss around the world, and we realized the importance of focusing on people as both the primary drivers of species extinction and as the best hope for preventing it. We have a tremendous opportunity to connect people to nature, reinforce environmental attitudes, and engage communities in conservation action."

The Call's strategic priority to IGNITE leveraged that potential to reach audiences worldwide, challenging us to awaken a global audience to take personal responsibility for the future of wildlife. Of course, this cannot be achieved by simply telling people what to do.

As symposium speaker Dr. Martha Monroe explained, "Effective programs are built with a knowledge of learning or behavior theory. The more we understand about what motivates people to engage in conservation actions, the better we can design programs to bridge the gaps and then evaluate whether or not we have affected the indicators of change."

"Planet Earth does not belong to the human race. The human race belongs to Planet Earth. I thoroughly enjoy what I do, and I feel very lucky that I get to be part of the fight to end extinction."
—*Dr. Pat Morris, associate director of veterinary services*

THE POWER OF STORY IN STRATEGIC MANAGEMENT

"Sometimes reality is too complex. Stories give it form."
Jean-Luc Godard, film director

Some years back, our CEO, Doug Myers, and several staff members from San Diego Zoo Global heard author and communications expert Andy Goodman speak at a conference. Andy, the director of The Goodman Center, spoke about the value of stories—not only to help people connect to information but also to remember it.

Andy has traveled across the United States and around the world for 15 years, talking to groups and organizations about the importance of telling stories. He has led more than 500 workshops, working with diverse groups such as First Nations tribal leaders in British Columbia, students at the African Leadership University in Mauritius, and forest conservation advocates in Thailand and Vietnam.

"Stories are the single most powerful communication tool you possess," Andy said to the room full of business leaders. "They engage an audience and inspire action."

Doug and the other leaders at SDZG were captivated—and convinced. Returning home from the conference, Doug prepared for a talk to a group of longtime SDZG supporters. As he looked at the PowerPoint slides he had created for the talk, he suddenly found them lacking. "What story could I tell that would energize this presentation?" Doug wondered. His talking points focused on SDZG's worldwide conservation efforts, including a brief mention of a new California condor hatchling in the wild. Using the storytelling principles Andy had outlined, Doug refocused his presentation to talk about the plight of these majestic birds. In essence, here's the story he told:

"California condors are the largest flying birds in North America, with a wingspan of nearly 10 feet. Native Americans call them thunderbirds, believing they bring thunder to the skies with the beating of their powerful wings. California condors used to range from British Columbia to northern Baja California, Mexico. Over time, however, the species became imperiled. California condor populations declined to just 22 individuals in the early 1980s. In 1986, the US Fish and Wildlife Service captured the remaining birds from the wild, placing them all in a managed care setting in hopes of breeding the birds so that we could eventually have a population large enough to release them back into the wild.

"The first chick conceived at a zoological facility hatched at the San Diego Zoo Safari Park in 1988. It was fed with a puppet that looked like an adult condor so the chick wouldn't bond to its human caretakers. Through careful breeding by the Safari Park and its partners, there were finally enough chicks to release back into the wild in 1992.

"The birds that are part of the breeding program at the Safari Park live in a large behind-the-scenes area known as the 'Condorminium' with netted enclosures that encourage them to learn to fly and avoid power poles and other hazards. The keepers perfected the technique of double-clutching, or removing an egg from the condor nest and artificially incubating it so that the bird would lay another egg. This allowed twice as many condor chicks to be produced. Over time, the number of breeding sites expanded and the world's population of condors grew to nearly 500. The effort to restore these majestic birds has not been without challenges, ranging from lead poisoning from spent ammunition to accidental ingestion of microtrash. Despite this, today 300 of these birds are flying free in wilderness areas in California, Arizona, Utah, and Baja California, Mexico."

Elements of a Good Story

Doug's words provided context for the condor hatchling, bringing the story to life and serving as a framework for the rest of his talk. The presentation Doug gave resonated with his audience, but more importantly, it sparked a permanent change in the way he would deliver future messages. Since then, SDZG has engaged Andy Goodman on many occasions to provide storytelling workshops for our organization and our partners.

In a fundamental way, storytelling and planning are related. A good story—and a good strategic plan—defines relationships, a sequence of events, cause and effect, and the priority among items. Those elements are likely to be remembered as a complex whole. That likelihood—and a substantial amount of cognitive science—argues strongly for strategic planning through storytelling.

Storytelling is a skill that can be learned. As Andy Goodman explained, the most powerful stories answer six important questions:

- **Who is the story about?** To get into a story, the audience needs to meet someone to identify with or who will serve as a guide through the landscape of the narrative. No matter what the subject or message is, the first question in the audience's mind is always "Who is this story about?"
- **What do they want?** Once the audience knows who to focus on, their next question is "What does he or she want?" From the outset, it must be

clear what the main character desires. This gives the audience a reason to care about the outcome.

- **What stands in their way?** Humans bore easily. Within the first few paragraphs of the story, the speaker or writer has to make the audience wonder, "What happens next?" or "How is this going to turn out?" As the characters in the story pursue their goal, they must run into obstacles, surprises, or something that makes the audience sit up and take notice.

- **How do they respond?** What do the people in the story do when they encounter an obstacle? Do they turn tail and run? Lower their head and bash through the wall? Find a clever way around it? How they navigate these challenges reveals character and also compels the audience to wonder, "What would I do in that situation?"

- **What happens in the end?** Has the objective been reached, or has something else happened? Once it is established who the story is about and what they want, the speaker must eventually answer the question "Did the character get there or not?"

- **What does it mean?** When the final line is spoken, the audience should know exactly why they took this journey. In the end, this may be the most important question of all: "What was that story all about?"

A new breed of strategic plan requires a powerful communications tool. Stories are central to human intelligence and memory. Cognitive scientist William Calvin describes how people gradually acquire the ability to formulate plans through the stories they hear in childhood. From stories, he explains, a child learns to "imagine a course of action, imagine its effects on others, and decide whether or not to do it."[15]

For Doug, the story of the California condors not only left a stronger impression on his audience than a handful of PowerPoint slides but also communicated a larger message of SDZG's pivotal role in conservation.

The Power of Story

- A strategic plan needs to tell a compelling story to be remembered and to inspire action.

- The elements of stories—and strategic plans—define relationships, outline a sequence of events, establish cause and effect, and prioritize items. Those elements are likely to be remembered as a complex whole.

- A good story identifies a central character, explains what that character wants, identifies obstacles standing in the character's way, shows how the character responds to the obstacles, and reveals what happens in the end. Most importantly, it must convey meaning—the reason you are telling this story to your audience.

LIVING THE CALL

CONNECTING THE STRATEGIC
WITH THE OPERATIONAL

*"You've got to think about big things while you're doing small things, so
that all the small things go in the right direction."*
Alvin Toffler, author and futurist

One of the most common frustrations surrounding the art of strategic planning is confusing the operational plan (or "action plan") with the strategic plan. An operational plan is the tactical accompaniment to a strategic plan. It delineates how an organization will implement the strategies of the strategic plan.

At San Diego Zoo Global, we have learned to keep the strategic plan at a high level with a three- to five-year horizon, while updating the operational plan every year and tying it to our annual budget. It took time for us to come to terms with this, but once we did, we were able to outline the specific actions that would help us accomplish the strategic plan in a concrete, measurable, and real-time way.

Every tactic in an operating plan has SMART (Specific, Measurable, Achievable, Realistic, and Timebound) goals. In the past, we tried to apply these characteristics to our overarching strategies, but found it impossible to remain at the strategic level and still meet the criteria of the SMART goals. The ups and downs of our shifting environment and changes to our annual budget made it impossible to build long-term buy-in for a strategy that was a moving target.

To draft SDZG's operational plan, we created a New Perspectives Strategic Planning (NPSP) team. This group represented about 40 staff members from a broad spectrum of departments. Many of the team members had never been exposed to strategic planning. CEO Doug Myers wanted to incorporate fresh thinking into the planning process as much as he wanted to include the institutional knowledge represented by the executives. It was a good blend of experience and innovation.

The team's primary function was to participate in structured, facilitated planning sessions where members would gather and synthesize information from the environmental scans, test the draft strategic plan, and craft the annual operational plan. Members were expected to:

- Participate in gathering information for the environmental scan
- Attend environmental scan presentations and capture the implications for SDZG
- Read and report on relevant literature to ensure that the NPSP team shared a collective base of knowledge
- Provide feedback on drafts of The Call by infusing it with realistic input from their areas of expertise
- Engage in discussion and projects with other NPSP team members to provide cross-functional input to each phase of the plan's development
- Brainstorm ideas for The Call's operational plan
- Assist in launching The Call by presenting the plan to audiences, reporting departmental success, and participating in the crucial first 100 days of implementation

- Ensure that The Call became a key component of the work done within each member's own department and teams
- Advocate for the vision throughout every step of the process

The NPSP group met several times over a six-month period, completing assignments in between. The team provided key input and unflinching feedback, which led to a more robust and realistic strategic plan.

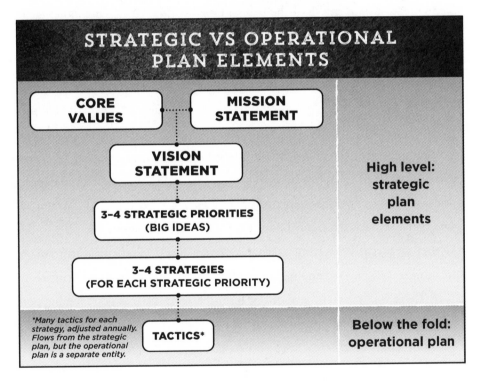

The Best of Both Worlds

Robin Keith, associate director of Vision, Innovation, and Strategy (VIS), facilitated the process. When she realized that the NPSP team was having difficulty translating their ideas into the actual operational plan itself, "I was surprised and a little disappointed at first. But I realized that the NPSP team could not create the operational plan without more input from the executive staff members, who would be critical in aligning resource allocation with the plan."

As with most operational plans, it became an iterative process. Robin took the raw material from the NPSP team and met with each member of the executive staff. She shared drafts with both the NPSP and the executive staff to make sure she was capturing the nuances of each team. Ultimately, she was able to create a plan that had the best of both worlds. "It was a balancing act that we tweaked over time," she said. "The resulting operational plan reflected a lot of the enthusiasm of the NPSP, but it was tempered with executive staff expert opinion to ensure that it could be successfully implemented."

NPSP member Katie Cox, a human resources benefits specialist, appreciated being involved early in the process. "Being on the NPSP team made us into champions for the plan while it was still in progress," she said. "We were buying into the plan on our own. We would return to our individual departments, where we not only explained the plan but lived it as well. When we would get feedback from our board and executive staff about the plan, it felt like they were really listening to what we had to say. It challenged us to make sure our ideas were good enough and bold enough, and it was an exciting team effort. There was a certain amount of humility to it all. It was such a big part of my life and the most significant thing I've done in my career. I'm lucky that I got to be a part of it!"

Architecture for Execution

Once SDZG had created the operational plan, we needed to implement it. In many organizations, the implementation phase is where strategic plans go to die. The implementation architecture for our 20th-century plans was weak— one of the primary reasons that our previous plans were not very transformational. Hundreds of pages filled a binder, listing a person's name next to every action for years to come. It wasn't iterative, synergistic, or aligned with day-to-day work.

Strategic plans require a carefully designed execution and a strong structure to support them, though. Our three Lynx plans had relied on multifunctional teams that would take on projects and follow through for a calendar year. This was crucial during The Lynx years when our organizational culture had not caught up with our ambitions. Once the executive staff began to embrace and finally own the plan, we were able to transition to a new architecture where the leaders of the organization would be held accountable for the plan's execution.

In contrast to The Lynx, the operational plan for The Call identifies every action needed to achieve each strategy, including dates and success metrics. This operational plan is reviewed every year for relevance and to ensure that it is actionable. While we don't change priorities for the three- to five-year life of our strategic plan, we recognize the need for a responsive operational plan that can be adjusted each year. (Operational items that require more than a year to implement are separated into multiple years, each with a portion of the accomplishment that is achievable within one year.)

The annual budget is tied to the operational plan, ensuring SDZG has the resources to move forward with any measures that require financial investment, personnel, or other expenditures. Because the operating plan is updated and measured annually and includes operational tactics tied to the organization's annual budget, our staff members are responsible for its implementation. Every action in The Call's operational plan has a specific due date and a person responsible for completing that work. At SDZG—as with many nonprofits—the operational plan does not go to the board for approval. Instead, the board approves the annual budget, which is made up of operational action items.

Although the strategic plan is shared with the staff, board, colleagues, donors, and others by request, the operational plan is the property of SDZG

Below the Fold: Plan Components

SDZG's operational plan consists of the following components:

- **A project-management reporting document,** such as a spreadsheet, Gantt project-management chart, or progress dashboards. It includes SMART goals and key success metrics. Each work group or department assigned to an action item completes a report and then the Vision, Innovation, and Strategy (VIS) group compiles all the reporting documents. This helps to quantify operational success throughout the year.

- **A comprehensive prose document** that lists all the tactics that have been proposed for the life span of the strategic plan. Many tactics are proposed during the strategic planning process but deemed too tactical for the strategic plan. Instead, these ideas are saved for consideration in the operational plan. Each tactic receives a discrete number that relates to the strategy it addresses. The VIS group keeps a historical record of every tactic that is completed, deleted, or changed throughout the plan as well as a copy of all products developed during the course of plan implementation. This helps to quantify success at the end of the plan's life.

- **Strategic plans for departments, work groups, or major internal initiatives.** Every executive staff member creates a strategic plan for their business unit to determine how their area's work will support The Call. Many of the action items in those internal strategic plans are taken from (or become) the tactics of the full plan. This helps to ensure alignment between the "day jobs" of staff and the progress of The Call.

staff and is not to be distributed outside of the organization. One reason for this is that the operational plan is meant to change often, so it would be confusing to have different versions circulating externally.

To remain flexible, SDZG constantly looks for new ways to implement the strategies of The Call. We have no qualms about deleting an action item if a better idea presents itself. As long as each action item has SMART goals aligned with The Call and the progress is routinely scrutinized, the operational plan can adapt to new ideas and fresh ways of thinking.

Here's an example of how the operational plan plays out in The Call. There are three strategies under the strategic priority of "UNITE." One strategy is to "inspire personal responsibility." The operational plan includes many actions under this strategy to provide the public with individual ways they can help wildlife. One of these actions was for SDZG to partner with TRAFFIC, the wildlife trade-monitoring network, and the Taronga Zoo in Australia to become its North American partner for a wildlife-trafficking app called Wildlife Witness. With this app, if travelers observe a potential wildlife trafficking incident, they can instantly report it via the app and the authorities will respond to it.

In essence, by creating clear action items to meet our larger goal of ending extinction, SDZG's operational plan functions as the workhorse for The Call.

STRATEGIC LEADERSHIP IN ACTION

"People buy into the leader before they buy into the vision."
John C. Maxwell, author and speaker

One of the most important lessons we learned in developing The Call was that each of us had to change if we wanted to achieve transformative results—that is, if we wanted to make real strides to end extinction. Whether it was our CEO, our chairman of the board, a manager, or a volunteer leading a committee . . . we all had to demonstrate that we were serious about improving our organization by substantially modifying the way we did business. At first, many of us thought this was someone else's responsibility or that we could change at some point later in the process, but we soon embraced making change that was truly real, deep, and meaningful.

And it started from the top. Our CEO, Doug Myers, had to change the way and the frequency with which he spoke about species conservation, the way he allocated resources, and the types of stories he shared with the board and staff. Doug's evolving attitudes and priorities—and his steadfast reinforcement of these in every meeting and budget allocation—showed stakeholders that he had changed, and he meant business.

As San Diego Zoo Global began to make changes in association with The Call, Doug's leadership style evolved to resemble what best-selling author Jim Collins calls a "level-5 leader." In his book *Good to Great,* Collins explains that all great organizations are headed by a level-5 leader.[16] These leaders have a unique combination of extreme personal humility combined with an intense personal will. This combination of modesty and fierce resolve resonates strongly with stakeholders and inspires dedicated followers.

"Over time, our CEO became a great example of a low-ego, high-value, principled leader," observed Dr. Don Janssen, retired corporate director of animal health at SDZG. "Doug began to empower the rest of us to do great things because we knew that he would have our back. He's now a master at this. He continually reinforces the idea that SDZG must choose to do the right thing, and to do it right. Because of this, people listen to him."

Doug consistently made decisions in accordance with these principles. He had to turn down many requests for resources that were not in alignment with the direction we had chosen. He insisted on giving credit to his team instead of taking the kudos for himself. And he supported the choices that his executives made, supporting our efforts to do the right thing. "Doug has evolved in many ways over the years," noted board member Cliff Hague. "Not many CEOs are capable of evolving like that."

Doug's example set the tone for other staff leaders. Dr. Bob Wiese, chief life sciences officer, recognized that working for the "greater organizational good" was vital to achieving a bold vision: "It required people to give up their self-interest in the fight for the cause. As we became better at strategic planning, more of our executives and managers were willing to sacrifice their own needs, and their individual department's needs, for SDZG's overall vision. This made more sense from a business perspective, but it had to be modeled from the top down."

Courage to Change

As the executive staff evolved, so did the board. SDZG's board members not only supported Doug, but they also became more focused on high-level strategy than short-term operational success. "I've lived in many places and been involved in organizations of all kinds. There are a lot of companies that are briefly successful and then are almost paralyzed in their inability to change," said board member Javade Chaudhri. "At SDZG, we came to embrace change, and we recognized that we needed to change. We developed the moral courage to do so."

This has been a huge accomplishment—particularly for an organization that is more than 100 years old. Prior to The Call, our corporate culture had overvalued tradition and stability. For instance, in the 20th century, each board member had been recruited for a lifetime seat on the small board (until mandatory retirement at age 75) with no financial commitment requested. This was a holdover from a time when the board of trustees was working to help supplement a meager staff. Most members were asked to join the board because their fathers had been on the board—as well as their grandfathers. It was difficult to move to a new way of doing business when we had that kind of a legacy to uphold.

Nevertheless, our board recognized that we needed new ways to bring SDZG into the 21st century. Board members were open to trying everything from new meeting schedules to a future-focused board succession plan. We learned that it was possible to respect the past *and* move toward the future.

Many of these ideas for change were sparked by a framework presented in *Governance as Leadership*.[17] The book advocates creating a pact between trustees and executives, with more macro-governance from the board—and less micromanagement—as well as a higher level of engagement from every board member.

The authors maintain that great governance includes fiduciary, strategic, and generative thinking. Fiduciary thinking is related to overseeing the resources of an organization. Strategic thinking is a way to get from the present state to a desired future state. And generative thinking focuses on the meaning behind the knowledge, information, and data—framing problems and making sense of issues while working toward generating new ideas. All of these modes are important, but most boards are mired in the fiduciary, have a hard time staying strategic, and rarely set foot in the generative mode.

To focus on all three modes—and thus propel our board forward—we made some key changes in board governance and practices. These included:

- **Beginning each board meeting with a "mission moment."** While the board covered many topics as outlined by the bylaws, we found that starting off with a five-minute example of how SDZG was making a difference reminded our board members why they were in the room and set a great tone for the rest of the meeting. For example, US Fish & Wildlife Service representatives visited one board meeting and talked about how our joint collaboration had helped with a desert tortoise crisis in Nevada. It was very moving for the board to hear firsthand about how this partnership affected the health and welfare of thousands of tortoises— including many that were able to return to the wild.

- **Adapting to meeting best practices.** It was hard to let go of "the way we've always done it." To help with this, our board meetings adopted a new framework that allowed time to address each mode of governance— fiduciary, strategic, and generative. The board members also adopted a consent agenda and cut down on routine presentations that could be handled via committee meetings or written reports. They even reduced the number of physical board meetings by half and offered a video option for board members who lived outside of San Diego County.

- **Including generative discussions on board agendas whenever time permitted.** The board's generative discussions invited creativity and exploration, but they did not end in a list of action steps or decisions.

Instead, they provided a forum for examining the organization and understanding others' viewpoints. These discussions allowed our board members to more fully make sense of the organization and its goals. Some generative prompts included:

- In five years, what will be most different about the board or how we govern?
- In 10 years, what's one thing that will be seen as the legacy of this board?
- What do you tell others about why you joined this board? When you first wake up in the morning, what do you tell yourself about why you are on this board? How are these different?

- **Ending board meetings with a "vision moment."** For SDZG, keeping the vision top of mind was key. The board often invited our scientists or animal and plant experts to tell a short story about their work. By celebrating a conservation success story or highlighting a problem for endangered plants and animals, the board was reminded of what our organization was working toward: to end extinction.

- **Aligning strategic planning efforts with council meetings.** A small number of councils, run jointly by the board and key staff members, addressed high-level SDZG issues. Each time the strategic plan changed, the councils were evaluated to ensure that they were still aligned with the strategic goals. For instance, a few years ago we had a conservation council, an animal health council, and a living collections council. As the organization moved toward a full-spectrum approach to species conservation, the three councils were combined into one conservation council. The councils used the strategic plan to identify and problem-solve strategic issues.

How Our Planning Roles Evolved

With any strategic plan, the roles of those involved in planning vary with an institution's culture as well as its bylaws. "In the past, the planning was driven by the board," recalled Berit Durler, SDZG's former board chair and trustee emeritus. "We came to see, however, that the role of the board was to set strategic direction and policies, but having staff input was vital because they would have to own the plan—from the CEO to the keepers and the scientists. We knew that if they didn't own it, they wouldn't execute it, no matter how great the plan. Now, our process is collaborative, but it is led by the executive staff."

Board member Cliff Hague agreed: "Now, when I work *with* the staff, as I did in helping develop strategic plans, I think of myself as an employee of the CEO and not a board member. When I provide other services to the staff, I'm providing counsel and advice and experience. You cannot expect that every idea you suggest is going to be acted upon; it's only going to provide intellectual capital."

The following table shows how SDZG used a RACI (Responsible, Accountable, Consulted, and Informed) matrix to help clarify the roles of staff, board members, and other key stakeholders in our strategic planning process. These roles vary for each organization, but for SDZG, it was a useful way to determine in advance what roles each group would play.

RACI MATRIX

PLANNING PHASE	Board	Executive staff leaders	Committee members	Staff members	External stakeholders
Mission, vision, and values	Accountable	Responsible	Consulted	Consulted	Informed
Determine priorities and strategies	Accountable	Responsible	Informed	Consulted	Informed
Operational plan (tactics)	Consulted	Accountable	Informed	Responsible	Informed
Financial plans	Accountable	Responsible	Informed	Informed	N/A
Other internal plans	Informed	Accountable	Informed	Responsible	Informed

For each row in the chart, we determined:

- **Responsible**: Which one person/group is responsible for completing the work?
- **Accountable**: Which one person/group is accountable for the decision (i.e., where does the buck stop)?
- **Consulted**: All people/groups who should be consulted before a decision or policy change is made.
- **Informed**: All people/groups who should be informed after a decision or policy change is made.

The RACI matrix also provided guidelines for other processes and projects. For example, the RACI matrix helped us work out some kinks in our system to design new animal habitats. Numerous staff members—including architects, animal-care experts, horticulturists, nutritionists, construction experts, zoo keepers, veterinarians, scientists, interpretation specialists, educators, financial professionals, fundraisers, and executives—had valuable perspectives to contribute. But although the staff groups were all involved, most of them didn't feel that the architects were keeping them in the loop as inevitable changes were made to the habitat plans. Meanwhile, the architects felt they were bending over backward to get input from everyone, but all they heard were complaints.

Most of these staff groups felt that they should be consulted before any changes were made to the habitat plans—but this just wasn't feasible in many cases. Therefore, we used the RACI matrix to tease out the crucial roles during each phase of the process: the preconstruction phase, the construction phase, and the post-construction phase (when animals and plants were introduced to the new habitat and maintenance work kicked in). During the preconstruction phase, it was important to get the input of the educators—so they were listed as "consulted." However, during the construction phase, it was impractical to consult educators before every decision, so they were listed as "informed."

Once the roles were established, it changed everyone's expectations. People knew that if they were listed as consulted, accountable, or responsible during new habitat development, they had the right and the obligation to weigh in on decisions. If they were listed as informed, they knew that they were not being asked for their opinion but were simply being updated on changes as they were made.

How We Changed

Undergoing a massive change doesn't happen overnight. At SDZG, it took many years and many people committed to transforming the organization.

First, we announced the change we wished to see in the world. There was power in the announcement, for us and for others. Once we had declared our intention, we reinforced the change with our actions. This wasn't easy; it was painful to change the way we had been doing things. But we realized that if it were easy, it wouldn't represent change and wouldn't demonstrate our commitment to the future.

Finally, when not everyone around us embraced the changes right away, we refused to be discouraged. We realized that in all likelihood, others were watching . . . and waiting to see if we really meant business. Similarly, we did not beat ourselves up (or worse, give up) when we failed to reinforce the new direction at every fork in the road. The important thing was to make decisions that were consistent with the change we envisioned over time.

About Strategic Leadership

- Strategic leadership begins with you. Demonstrating your steadfast belief in the process will inspire others to buy in as well.
- A thorough strategic planning process includes executive staff, board members, and other stakeholders—each with clearly defined roles.
- Your organization's bylaws and culture will dictate the responsibilities for those involved in the creation of a strategic plan, so it's important to document these roles at the start of the process.

MANAGING CHANGE

"A team aligned behind a vision will move mountains."
Kevin Rose, business tech entrepreneur

At San Diego Zoo Global, our culture of planning now extends to the department level, which includes the work of our scientists. During one session of departmental strategic planning, our scientists envisioned an exciting future for the San Diego Zoo Institute for Conservation Research that could have the potential to save many endangered species. But when the scientists examined the things that would have to change to achieve this desired future, they kept hitting a brick wall.

"There's no way we can achieve what we want because we can't get the support from our public relations department," one scientist said in frustration. "What good does it do for us to achieve scientific milestones if no one knows who we are or what we're doing?" Another scientist agreed: "That's right! If we can't get our stories shared with the rest of the world, we won't be able to get these important projects funded. I guess we'll have to set our sights lower."

It was true: in the past, our scientists hadn't always received the level of support they wanted from either our public relations team or SDZG's fundraising professionals. In fact, for the scientists this had been a critical stumbling block in previous strategic plans. Our public relations department had explained that they couldn't interest any news outlets in the complicated stories the scientists needed to tell. As the scientists discussed this during the department meeting, though, one of them pushed back: "Maybe we need to start asking ourselves why our story is not getting communicated. Perhaps we need to start focusing on more than just the future of our science. How much of this is within our control? How can *we* change to get our story told?"

A Long and Winding Road

After some initial frustration, the group started to consider this. Historically, the other departments sometimes had trouble understanding the significance of the complex scientific progress that was most meaningful to endangered animals and plants, but the scientists had always seen this as a failing of those other departments, rather than their own shortcoming.

The scientists soon realized they had it within their control to craft the best publicity story that SDZG had to tell. But this would require them to venture far from their comfort zone as they strove to tell their scientific stories to lay audiences in such a compelling way that other departments could not resist sharing them.

Over time, this revolutionized the dynamic between our experts and those who told their stories. Our scientists continued to explain complex issues to their scientific colleagues, of course, *and* they learned to share their stories in a way that others found understandable and exciting. Not only did it work for press releases and grant applications, but it was also revolutionary for the many staff members and volunteers who interacted with San Diego Zoo and San Diego Zoo Safari Park guests. And it all began with the scientists' realization that they themselves had to change before they could expect the world around them to change.

One of the hardest parts of any successful strategic effort is managing change. Most people want change to happen, but *they* don't want to change—they want someone else to change. Many groups talk about choosing a strategic plan that will "keep everyone happy." But true change always has a messy and uncomfortable phase. Commitment to the process is what gets organizations through difficult times.

As SDZG started down the path toward revolutionary change, we found that the processes we had agreed upon were challenged at every bend. We wanted to be open to new ideas and new ways of working, of course, but we had learned from experience that we would not realize major change by shifting our strategic planning process to make it easier on the staff, board, and volunteers. If we wanted to move mountains to end extinction, we should not expect it to be easy.

In fact, there were many times stakeholders rebelled against the changes put forth by The Call. Scientists who were excited about the new emphasis were nonetheless distressed to realize that the new focus would dictate the projects they could pursue. Board members who supported the concept were still skeptical of whether or not it was financially sustainable and were fearful of any financial downturn.

We were also tested when progress was halted or derailed at many key moments. Sometimes it was an element outside our control, like unseasonably bad weather during construction or new legislation that stalled a project. Sometimes it was an unanticipated consequence to the direction we had set that then required a course correction.

We realized it was important to recognize that there would be challenges. In short, success came down to our ability to trust the process we had agreed to—and to continuously work to align our activities with our strategic plan.

Achieving Greater Alignment

Once we felt more comfortable with trusting the process, we found the structure of The Call allowed us to see full alignment across all areas of our business. David Page, SDZG's corporate director of finance, recalled, "The Lynx moved us toward an integrated approach, but The Call has taken it a step further. It has a network of interconnected pieces that allows us to see a connection between every action of our jobs."

David noted that in the past, departments within SDZG only saw the work they did and could not understand why they couldn't have more resources if the organization was doing well. "Now," David said, "staff in the operations department can see how they are helping to end extinction. They can see that their work makes it possible for keepers to provide animal care so that guests can see animals, which connects to our financial well-being as an organization, which provides funds to end extinction. It's clear to everyone how they contribute to success."

This fundamental—and unprecedented—shift helped our staff align around a common goal. "We're no longer competing internally for resources," David explained. "We're focusing our resources toward the same goal."

MEASURING WHAT MATTERS

"In business, money is both an input and an output. In the social sectors,
money is only an input, and not a measure of greatness."
Jim Collins, author

As we lived out The Call, we discovered that what you use to measure success reveals what you genuinely value. For instance, San Diego Zoo Global needed to generate an enormous amount of revenue to care for the plants and animals of the San Diego Zoo and San Diego Zoo Safari Park as well as to funnel the proceeds back into conservation work. We realized, however, if revenue was our major measure of success, it would put pressure on our organization to bring in revenue at all costs. Although elements such as animal welfare and conservation value were much more difficult to quantify, they were crucial to the success of The Call and SDZG's organizational values.

Best-selling author Jim Collins explains this concept well. After publishing *Good to Great*, Collins realized that some of the key concepts in the book did not address the unique challenges of nonprofit organizations. He wrote a monograph called *Good to Great and the Social Sectors* to serve as a companion piece to *Good to Great*. The monograph points out one key difference between nonprofit organizations and for-profit organizations.[18] "In business," he wrote, "money is both an input (a resource for achieving greatness) *and* an output (a measure of greatness). In the social sectors, money is *only* an input, and not a measure of greatness."

In other words, for-profit companies take in money (input) so they can make even more money (output) for their shareholders. Not-for-profit organizations or associations, such as SDZG, must take in money (input) to do more to solve the world's problems (output). Nonprofits need money, of course, but they are required to put it back into their organizations to continue to provide output in the form of mission realization.

Jim Collins points out that a great organization is one that delivers superior performance and makes a distinctive impact over a long period of time. "In the social sectors," he wrote, "the critical question is not 'How much money do we make per dollar of invested capital?' but 'How effectively do we deliver on our mission and make a distinctive impact relative to our resources?'"

Here's an example of how this plays out. The charts that follow include revenue and expense lines for two successful organizations. The first chart illustrates a for-profit company. In that model, the revenue (top line) increases, but the expenses (bottom line) remain relatively unchanged. The gap between the top line and the bottom line represents the amount of profit returned to shareholders.

The second chart illustrates a thriving nonprofit organizational construct. This time, as the revenue increases, money is put back into the organization, allowing it to do even more to deliver on its mission. With the nonprofit, the gap is much smaller between revenue and expenses. The revenue still needs to continue to improve over time if the organization is to continue to deliver on its good works, such as striving to end extinction. The revenue provides the nonprofit with money for expenses that are related to delivering on its mission and bringing its vision to life.

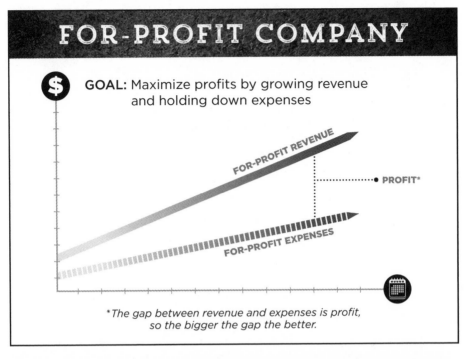

FOR-PROFIT COMPANY

$ GOAL: Maximize profits by growing revenue and holding down expenses

FOR-PROFIT REVENUE

• PROFIT*

FOR-PROFIT EXPENSES

The gap between revenue and expenses is profit, so the bigger the gap the better.

NONPROFIT ORGANIZATION

$ GOAL: Maximize mission activities by reinvesting most excess revenue back into the nonprofit's cause

NONPROFIT REVENUE

EXCESS REVENUE OVER EXPENSES*

NONPROFIT EXPENSES

A small gap between revenue and expenses ensures sustainability while allowing for maximum Return On Mission (ROM).

ROM and ROI

At SDZG, we used a four-quadrant tool to make decisions centered on comparing the Return On Mission (ROM) while examining the Return On Investment (ROI), particularly when considering a new initiative. Our early strategic conflicts centered around this concept. During The Lynx years, as we wrestled with dual goals of saving wildlife and providing recreation, we struggled with deciding between the many competing opportunities presented to us.

An example of this tension occurred when a four-dimensional (4D) theater was installed at the San Diego Zoo Safari Park. The theater came equipped with a movie about a popular cartoon character. The theater was clearly a revenue-generating opportunity for families to have fun at the Safari Park, which was within the scope of our mission at the time. Yet we weren't sure how this theater—a popular revenue-generating experience—would move us toward our vision, which at the time was to become a world leader at connecting people to wildlife and conservation.

When we came upon conflicts like this, our leaders evaluated them based on a simple 2 x 2 matrix we called "ROM vs ROI" that helped plot our options. The 4D theater fit into Quadrant D: although it did not directly move the needle on the mission and vision, it made money, which could be put toward moving the mission and vision forward.

ROM vs ROI

RETURN ON MISSION (ROM)	Quadrant **B** High ROM; Low ROI (Unsustainable)	Quadrant **A** High ROM; High ROI (Best fit!)
	Quadrant **C** Low ROM; Low ROI (No value)	Quadrant **D** Low ROM; High ROI (Profitable distraction)
	RETURN ON INVESTMENT (ROI)	

This matrix is not meant to do the hard work of saying yes or no to potential initiatives. It is simply a structured way to have a dialogue about the relative merit of various options. The results are not black or white.

We've found that instead of deciding whether or not an initiative is a good fit for us, it's better to ask, "How could this profitable distraction move into an upper quadrant with increased ROM?" In the theater example, SDZG was able to find a movie that was both popular and told conservation stories, which bumped it into the home run category of Quadrant A.

What to Measure

At SDZG, we view revenue, funding, margins, and other typical financial metrics as crucial gauges for success because they are essential to maintaining a healthy, sustainable business model. We also consider the number of guests to our Zoo, Safari Park, or our websites as Key Performance Indicators (KPIs)— also called Key Performance Metrics—since each visitor provides an opportunity for us to ignite his or her passion for wildlife.

But after launching The Call, we needed to identify additional new metrics to ensure we would be successful in leading the fight against extinction. We examined various measures that might capture this, but all had a fundamental flaw: the metrics did not provide a meaningful way to measure our impact.

If we had set any of the following metrics as performance goals, we realized that we would be measuring outputs rather than outcomes. For example:

- **We realized that measuring the number of species with which we were working on conservation solutions did not provide a meaningful KPI** because it wouldn't be useful to raise or lower that number year over year. We wanted to deepen the impact on species, not just create a longer laundry list of species we were helping. As time went on, this turned out to be true: we were working with 230 species in 2014, but by 2017 we had winnowed this to 215 species for which we could provide a deeper impact.

- **We also didn't want to use population size as a KPI,** since some species could have a relatively small number of individuals and still be viable, while other species would need large herds or flocks to remain genetically and demographically healthy.

- **For similar reasons, we couldn't use the number of individuals that have produced offspring** as a valid annual goal. Elephants, for example, take 22 months to gestate a calf, while some possums can produce offspring in just 12 days. And certain individual animals have birth control measures employed because they are genetically overrepresented.

- **Finally, although we wanted to increase collaboration, we realized it was not valuable for us to track the number of partners.** The goal was not to randomly add collaborators to lengthen the list but to seek out collaborators who could fill a complementary niche that would help species in a way that we could not.

After determining what *not* to measure, we tasked our scientists, veterinarians, and husbandry experts with developing a way to measure what really matters to The Call. They came up with a full-spectrum approach that matched each of our priority species with a set of key needs that must be met to ensure its survival. With this approach, SDZG can then assess the degree to which those needs are currently being met by our organization or one of our collaborators. Any needs that are not being addressed are flagged as a gap in the full-spectrum matrix.

For example, SDZG has been working with the Chinese government and scientists on releasing giant pandas into the wild; in fact, we are the only foreign entity allowed to work on the project. We also provide expertise and help with species care and management as well as scientific research. However, we do not advocate for legislation or provide habitat, public engagement, and post-release population support because other entities are serving those needs.

This approach identifies the gaps in the overall approach to conservation of each priority species. We believe tracking the number of priority species with gaps in their action plans will be a useful metric for genuine conservation progress. Each year, we aim to have fewer gaps in the full-spectrum matrix for our priority species. As with any scientific metric, it will take three to four years of results to determine if this is a viable KPI, but creating new metrics that measure impact relative to our mission and vision is essential to helping SDZG become a conservation organization that can lead the fight against extinction.

Measuring Internal Adoption

In addition to crafting meaningful external measures, we also historically measure a plan's adoption within our organization. For instance, each year we track our strategic plan's traction with staff and volunteer satisfaction and engagement surveys. Our internal surveys include two key statements related to overall mission and purpose. The first statement is "I am familiar with and understand the direction San Diego Zoo Global is heading with the strategic plan (The Call)." The second is "The management staff within my department provides regular information about the San Diego Zoo Global strategic plan (The Call) and the goals of the organization."

The responses to these two statements allow us to track our engagement score year over year. A score of 33–66 falls between "somewhat disagreeing" and "somewhat agreeing." A score above 66 means that the average score was either "somewhat agreeing" or "strongly agreeing."

The annual satisfaction survey began as an action item of The Lynx. For most of the years that The Lynx strategic plans were in play, our staff and volunteers' understanding of the plan hovered around a score of 65 to 68, or "somewhat agreeing." In 2014, SDZG had a gap year as we completed the last of The Lynx action items and worked on creating The Call. This involved mostly

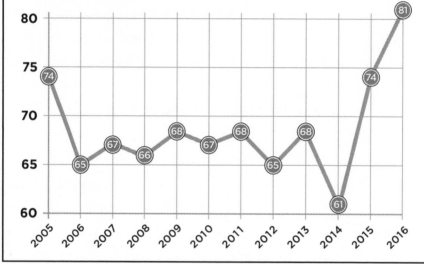

SAN DIEGO ZOO GLOBAL EMPLOYEE SATISFACTION SURVEY

1. I am familiar with and understand the direction San Diego Zoo Global is heading with the strategic plan (The Call).

finishing our punch list and conducting strategic planning activities, so there was little to report until The Call was completed. During this gap year, according to the surveys, our employees' engagement with the plan dipped to an all-time low score of 61.

When The Call strategic plan was launched in mid-2015, it clearly resonated with employees from the beginning. The score for familiarity with and understanding of The Call shot up to an unprecedented 81 after The Call's first full year of implementation. With nearly 3,000 employees at SDZG (and more than 90 percent participating), it is hard to achieve a bump of even a couple of points in a year—so the jump in data was very telling.

For SDZG, these surveys have been invaluable, providing much-needed

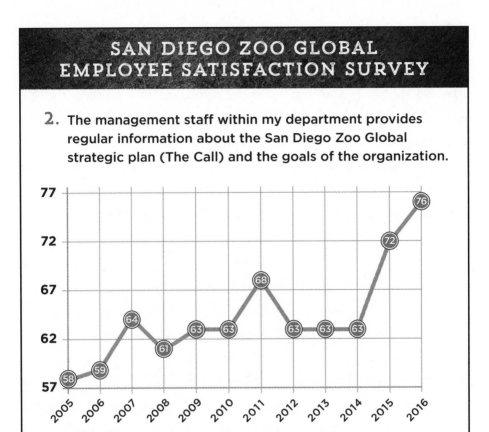

SAN DIEGO ZOO GLOBAL EMPLOYEE SATISFACTION SURVEY

2. The management staff within my department provides regular information about the San Diego Zoo Global strategic plan (The Call) and the goals of the organization.

information about one of our most important KPIs: our employees and the degree to which they have embraced our strategic plans.

Straight from the Boss

Over the years, SDZG has asked our employees how they would like to hear about the organization's goals. Would they prefer to hear the goals from our CEO, or would they rather read about them in a newsletter or on a bulletin board? Time and again, staff members have said that they want to hear about the goals directly from their own manager. Managers can explain how a goal relates to their employees, and staff members will take their cue about each goal's genuine importance from their managers.

When SDZG conducted our first employee survey in 2005, our managers did not yet see it as their role to communicate the organization's goals. When asked whether management staff provided regular information about the strategic plan, employees responded with a low score, hovering between "somewhat disagreeing" and "somewhat agreeing."

As we mentioned before, it's hard to move thousands of people up the scale very far or very fast, but the action items from The Lynx strategic and operational plans encouraged managers to rise to the challenge. Many of the action items specifically called for increased inter- and intradepartmental communication. Our managers began to communicate with their departments about The Lynx, maintaining a steady level of discussion throughout the years.

Unlike The Lynx, The Call quickly gained traction among both the staff and their managers because it represented a bold and exciting new direction that everyone was proud to pursue. Supervisors were able to see much more clearly how The Call strategic plan related to the work of their department, and all employees had a new enthusiasm for the plan. When asked how well managers were communicating SDZG's plan, employees responded with an amazing jump, going from a score of 63 in 2014 to 76 in 2016.

These annual measurements of how well our staff understands and cares about the strategic plan have become important Key Performance Indicators (KPIs). Today, groups or colleagues who visit the Zoo or Safari Park are encouraged to ask our employees about The Call. We find that about 80 percent of the employees and volunteers who interact with guests will be able to articulate the fundamental elements of The Call. This means that the 16-year-old staffer who rents a guest a stroller at the San Diego Zoo will be able to explain that The Call is our plan to lead the fight against extinction!

About Strategic Planning Metrics

- What you use to determine success is very telling about what your organization genuinely values. If revenue is the only key measure of success in a mission-driven organization, it will pressure staff to bring in revenue at all costs.

- The ways in which you deliver on your mission are much more difficult to quantify than revenue, so it is easy to declare those metrics as impossible to measure. However, they are as crucial to your success as your financial results.

- A simple way to evaluate potential new initiatives is to look at the Return On Investment (ROI) in tandem with the Return On Mission/Vision (ROM). The best-choice initiatives will offer a return in both ways: a positive financial outcome coupled with a strong move toward your mission and vision.

TEACHING PEOPLE
HOW TO SAY NO

"The essence of strategy is choosing what not to do."
Michael Porter, economist, researcher, and author

The leaders of San Diego Zoo Global's development and membership department loved the idea of The Call, but they couldn't imagine how they would implement it. They gathered in the San Diego Zoo's Panda Conference Room, a space designed to spark creativity that included a view of a panda munching on bamboo from a nearby tree. Mark Stuart, our chief development and membership officer, had invited his top team to the meeting and asked each person to bring a list of all his or her current activities, programs, and plans.

Mark challenged the group members to think about how their department could help The Call. Enthusiastic about this new direction and what it would mean for the future of animals, the development and membership leaders quickly generated dozens of ideas. Next, they synthesized their department's role in relation to The Call. They agreed that their best contribution would be providing resources that the organization couldn't generate through tickets or merchandise. To achieve the strategies set out in The Call, they would aim to raise significantly more money: from their current total of $30 million per year to $50 million per year.

The group realized that this new level of fundraising could fuel our fight against extinction. The energy in the room was palpable as the group considered this. But gradually, a hush fell over the room as the leaders looked down at their list of current activities.

"I'm excited about the direction we're going," commented one frustrated fundraising professional as she studied her list, "but I'm already about to go underwater with my current workload. How can I possibly raise even more money? How can I add conservation-related fundraising activities to my plate?" Heads nodded around the room.

You Make The Call

Mark was prepared for this response. He unveiled a tool that the executives had created to help solve this problem, called the "Make The Call" canvas. The canvas was a simple 2 x 2 matrix with four quadrants labeled:

- **Swans:** programs or activities that aligned best with The Call
- **Ugly ducklings:** activities that were well aligned but needed some work before they could evolve into swans
- **Sacred cows:** programs that must continue for reasons beyond our control, such as fulfilling a grant we had received before we created The Call
- **Crabgrass:** activities that were not as aligned with The Call as others on the list

The leaders in the room represented seven areas of the department, so Mark gave each area its own canvas. He asked the group members to write the names of their programs and activities on yellow sticky notes (one program per note) and place them in the category they felt would be the best fit. Eagerly, they applied their notes to their canvases. Every canvas had many swans. A few groups had put some programs in the sacred cow or ugly duckling categories. The crabgrass section, however, remained empty on every canvas.

Next, the group members took pink sticky notes and wrote the names of all the new programs or activities the group had brainstormed earlier in the day. They were excited about adding these programs to the canvas, and—since they had just come up with them—they quickly put most of them in the swan quadrant. Between the yellow and the pink sticky notes, the swan quadrants were brimming with notes layered one on top of each other.

Then Mark said, "It's a given that all the activities you're currently working on are good programs, or you would have given them up a long time ago. The purpose of this exercise, though, is to figure out which ones are the best fit with our new strategic plan and the ambitious goals needed to fund them. Hopefully this will also allow us to implement some of these new ideas. Let's separate the good from the great by redistributing your sticky notes across the canvas. This time, each quadrant must have an equal number of programs."

Nobody moved. They stared at their canvases, then at Mark. "None of my activities are crabgrass," said one confused manager. "We can't just quit doing any of the initiatives I work on. Donors would be very unhappy if we stopped any of the things I see on my canvas."

"No one is saying that we'll stop doing anything at this point," Mark replied. "Let's just take a hard look at which programs are best aligned in relation to the others."

The group members reluctantly began to shift the notes around on their canvases.

Gradually, the sacred cow areas were filled with donor events that took an enormous amount of staff time and produced little revenue, grant applications that no longer represented the type of work we wanted to be known for, and work done for a small group of members at the expense of a larger group. The ugly duckling quadrants were populated with programs that the department had wanted to fine-tune but hadn't had time.

No one wanted to put anything in their crabgrass quadrant, but because Mark had asked them to spread their notes equally among the four quadrants, they reluctantly plucked notes from other areas and relocated them. Everyone was quietly reflective during this part of the exercise. "Well, if I had to put *anything* in the crabgrass section, it would be this program," said an associate director. "It requires much more effort than it yields."

Once people began to put items in the crabgrass quadrant, no matter how reluctantly, a curious thing happened. They started to see those projects in a different light. The staff began to imagine how much they could accomplish if their crabgrass programs could be phased out and, eventually, eliminated completely. Although Mark had said they didn't have to think about stopping things, the managers began to discuss this on their own. The tone of the conversation changed as people began to realize that Mark was giving them the power to think differently about the work they were doing. Then Mark challenged his team to look at items in all quadrants and think about what it would take to shift them to become swans.

Starting the Conversation

The idea behind the Make The Call exercise was to prompt a conversation between the supervisors and their staff after the meeting. It gave everyone the power to "make the call" about what they could stop doing—providing they could demonstrate to their supervisors that the new activity would help achieve the strategic priorities better than the old one.

"As we started looking at the Make The Call canvas," Mark noted, "it forced us to examine everything we were doing. It helped us make some tough decisions. It created a collaborative and safe environment for our discussions

MAKE THE CALL ALIGNMENT TOOL

Sacred COW

Sacred Cows are programs required for reasons beyond our control, but that doesn't mean that we shouldn't evaluate ways to make them a better fit.

Cows are untouchable.

Criteria for this category:

- Perceived to be untouchable
- Required for reasons outside the control of the implementers

Examples:

- Needed to fulfill a grant that is no longer optimally mission/vision aligned
- Historical precedent or partner relationships require that we maintain the program
- Perception that the program must continue because "we've always done it this way"

SWAN Synergy

Swans are the best of the best. They meet our goals; they align with our plans. What can we do to make these Swans even better?

Swans are home runs!

Criteria for this category:

- Aligns with and advances The Call
- Allows us to work in our niche
- Rises to the top of other programs in our control
- It is in our target area of expertise ... we are the best-suited organization/department to take on this program

Examples:

- High ROM and ROI
- Sustainable funding source in place
- Maximizes internal/external collaboration and synergy

CRAB Grass

Crabgrass is an invasive species and therefore representative of something we would be better off without.

Crabgrass is least aligned.

Criteria for this category:

- Does not align with The Call as well as comparable programs
- Does not meet relevant goals as well as similar programs
- Has lower ROM than other programs

Examples:

- Does not have sustainable funding
- Lacks opportunities for collaboration and synergy
- Is solely revenue-driven and not mission/vision aligned

Ugly DUCKLING

Ugly Ducklings have the potential to turn into Swans, but only if significant adjustments are made to achieve better alignment.

Ducklings need work.

Criteria for this category:

- Other programs are more aligned than these
- These are likely to be good programs, but they are not as great as other programs

Examples:

- No sustainable funding source
- Unrealized potential for collaboration and synergy
- Needs tweaking in terms of ROM and/or ROI to become a Swan

and showed what we could live without." Mark said they found that many activities they had done for decades just weren't yielding results in the current environment. "We had to admit that the juice wasn't worth the squeeze," he commented. "Now we are careful to ask ourselves if we are doing something that worked for our donors years ago but no longer resonates with our current supporters. The Make The Call canvas helped us create an exit plan for events or initiatives that were no longer moving us forward."

Deciding what to eliminate from our workload—not just in the development and membership department but throughout the organization—was a tough part of getting alignment with our new strategic plan. But it also offered us opportunities to discuss trade-offs with various departments, such as membership and development, and helped them deepen their understanding of their role in The Call.

"The Call has helped me to reevaluate and better align my priorities with those of SDZG," noted Dr. Meg Sutherland-Smith, Zoo director of veterinary services. "It has acted as a guiding light as well as an inspiration for what we do on a daily basis."

Mission Drift

Like many nonprofit organizations and associations, we were particularly susceptible to the lure of wanting to do it all. There would always be more plants and animals in need than we could help, and we couldn't imagine that we would stop doing anything that benefited our cause. And yet we had only so many resources. Therefore, we realized that the best way to serve the world's animals and plants was by targeting our efforts to make the most of those resources. This meant that we would have to say no to many things to do more of what we had determined was in our niche.

We understood that if everything seemed to fit within our mission and vision, this was a sign that the mission and vision needed tightening. For

SDZG, the value of our mission and vision statements is as much about helping us decide what *not* to do as it is in leading us to specific activities. These
well-crafted statements have helped us make decisions about what is—and is
not—within the scope of our dreams.

Under this structure, it quickly became obvious that some programs or
projects we wanted to do either would not fit under the umbrella of our mission or would not help us achieve our vision. This felt incredibly frustrating,
particularly when we knew we could garner significant financial support for
the ideas. But we realized it would be a slippery slope to tell ourselves that
the ideas we wanted to pursue—those ideas that were just outside the edge of
our mission—would make enough money to fund a lot of good work that was
within our mission. If we did that, then where would we stop? This phenom-
enon is called *mission drift*, and it is a particularly dangerous impediment to
bringing an organization's vision to life.

We were confronted with an example of mission drift a few years ago
when a corporate sponsor proposed installing a tall, iconic statue of a piece
of pasta at the entrance to the San Diego Zoo. The well-meaning sponsor
knew it would be a playful way to call attention to their signature noodle
product and would be seen by millions of families each year, so the sponsor
was willing to pay an exorbitant fee in exchange for the installation of the
statue. It was a tough choice because the pasta statue wasn't in direct opposi-
tion to our mission, and SDZG could do a lot of good for conservation with
the fees we would receive. It was a "shiny object," though—an opportunistic
distraction from our purpose that would dilute our mission in the eyes of our
guests. Ultimately, we passed on the statue because it was not going to propel
us toward our vision.

Pursuing ideas that were outside our mission but fundable (or revenue generators) were profitable distractions. They not only kept us from
moving toward our vision of ending extinction, but they also cost us other

opportunities. Spending resources on a project outside our strategy meant that we were diverting time and/or money from achieving our vision.

Once we accepted this, it got much easier to say no.

About Saying No

- Everyone wants change, but nobody wants to change his or her own behavior. This is human nature.
- Work that yields a reward but does not take you in the direction of your vision is called a profitable distraction. While these sometimes seem innocuous or even essential, they represent a slippery slope.
- You cannot take on the work identified in a new strategic plan until you can let go of the misaligned work in which you are already invested.

HOW THE CALL CHANGED US

"The next time you are looking at a charity, don't ask about the rate of their overhead. Ask about the scale of their dreams."
Dan Pallotta, entrepreneur and humanitarian

The Call helped us to bring focus to our organization and unity of purpose to our board, staff, and volunteers. We still have plenty of work to do, but we are well on our way toward fulfilling our dream of leading the fight against extinction.

One of the most critical outcomes of The Call was our recognition that to truly lead the fight against extinction, San Diego Zoo Global must not only do good work but also facilitate collaborative conservation, assembling and coordinating the unique set of skills required to save species. To achieve the vision we aspire to, we must find new models of collaboration that can deliver long-term impact.

For a long time, we had been compelled to do more for local species, but we had trouble finding the niche in which we could help the most. "I remember reading a book by David Hancocks in 2001," recalled Dr. Allison Alberts, SDZG's chief conservation and research officer. "It was called *A Different*

Nature: The Paradoxical World of Zoos and Their Uncertain Future.[19] It portrayed us in a less than flattering light."

In his book, Hancocks says, "Visitors to the San Diego Zoo can hear messages about the threat of tiger extinction and nod their head in concern, and then drive north to the San Diego [Zoo Safari Park] and hear messages about the depredation of elephants by poaching and comfort themselves by agreeing that they will never purchase ivory. The road they will have traveled between these sister zoos will have carried them through a region in which virtually every square inch of native chaparral habitat has been destroyed. It has been replaced by suburban sprawl and monoculture farms. Southern California contains one-fourth of all plant species known in the United States, half of them found nowhere else in the world, and it is one of the most endangered ecosystems on earth. Yet there will be no hint from these two Southern California zoos revealing this problem."

Allison was struck by this assertion. "Painful as it was to read, it was basically true," she said. "I remember thinking that it wasn't even just about our messaging but about the focus of our conservation work as well. For me, this was the seed of an idea that would eventually lead to a strategy in our previous strategic plan, The Lynx, compelling us to seek to become the conservation leader of the Southwest—indeed, [I felt] that we were obligated to do so."

SDZG began work on a series of conservation projects with local species, including the cactus wren, the pocket mouse, the mountain yellow-legged frog, and a host of native plant species. "With a lot of hard work by many people," Allison reported, "we made the shift and are now widely regarded as successful conservation leaders in the Southwest." Although it was still a focused effort due to SDZG's limited resources, this represented an enormous swing for our organization.

Then, a group of SDZG staff leaders visited Australia, where they saw a thriving collective-impact approach to halting extinction. Melbourne's

Zoos Victoria, in particular, was committed to saving local species from extinction, and there was a continent-wide effort to save native species, with many disparate conservation players working together. Mark Stuart, SDZG's chief development and membership officer, was on the trip. "We had an immediate 'aha' moment," he recalled. "San Diego is the most biologically rich county in the continental United States. It is also the most biologically threatened county, with approximately 200 imperiled plant and animal species. We realized we needed to follow the Zoos Victoria example and lead the fight to save all the indigenous species in our own backyard."

The difference, the leaders realized, was that SDZG would need to bring together many key players in San Diego County to pull this off. San Diego is home to numerous organizations committed to addressing habitat loss and species extinction, so it seemed like a perfect fit.

"The idea of bringing local organizations together to unite around the common goal of fighting extinction in San Diego County quickly gained momentum," recalled Robin Keith, associate director of Vision, Innovation, and Strategy. "In 2016, the San Diego End Extinction [SDEE] initiative was born. We served as facilitators of the effort, bringing together partners from private, public, and nonprofit sectors."

Rather than focusing on saving individual species, this initiative seeks to agree on a shared vision for conservation solutions that can be applied to all endangered animals, plants, and habitats throughout the county. SDZG's initial founding partners in the SDEE effort include those with land management responsibility: the County of San Diego Department of Parks and Recreation, the US Fish and Wildlife Service, the US Forest Service, the US Navy, the US Department of Defense, the US Geological Survey, San Diego County Supervisor Ron Roberts, the San Diego Association of Governments, the San Diego Foundation, the San Diego County Farm Bureau, and the California Department of Fish and Wildlife. The next step will be to engage a suite of local conservation organizations as key action partners.

The SDEE initiative goes beyond the barriers of individual entities to leverage collaboration as a springboard to collective impact. "It is our hope that no local species will go extinct on our watch," Robin said, "and that this collaboration can become a model for counties across the United States."

Dr. Allison Alberts agreed: "Our work to become the conservation leader in the Southwest during The Lynx put us in an ideal position to lead the SDEE effort as part of The Call. I believe that our shift toward saving local species is one of our greatest organizational success stories."

A Focus on Wildlife Trafficking

Another key area of progress has been reducing wildlife trafficking, the illegal collection, transport, and/or sale of plants and animals (alive or dead) and their parts. Consumers use these materials for food, the pet trade, traditional medicine, trophies, decorations, luxury status symbols, and private collections. While trade in sustainably collected, non-endangered wildlife is often legal, it is usually the rarest animals and plants that are in greatest demand, which drives the black market's huge profits and propels wildlife trafficking.

Some wildlife trade is both legal and sustainable; examples include alligator farming, legal timber harvesting, and permitted animal and plant collection for conservation and development of sustainable assurance populations. Legal subsistence hunting, gathering, fishing, and other collection activities that local people engage in for the purpose of securing resources for their family's use and survival are not defined as wildlife trafficking.

Illegal trade in wildlife occurs when local and international laws are broken for the purpose of commercial enterprise. Often, these laws support CITES—the Convention on International Trade in Endangered Species of Wild Fauna and Flora—an agreement between governments to ensure that international trade of wild animals and plants does not threaten species survival. Typically, laws are broken when that commerce proves exceptionally lucrative, as is the case for species like elephants and rhinoceroses. Unfortunately, elephant ivory and rhino horns can bring big financial returns for poachers and the crime syndicates that fund them. Ounce for ounce, rhino horn is worth more than drugs like cocaine on the black market, drawing as much as $132,000 per pound.

This is the primary reason that rhino populations are suddenly experiencing steep declines. In 2017, poachers slaughtered more than 1,000 rhinos across the globe. "That's one rhino killed nearly every eight hours for the purpose of making money for criminal organizations," noted Suzanne Hall, conservation policy specialist for SDZG. At that rate, rhinos could be extinct within 15 years. And elephants are victims, too, drawing closer to the threat of extinction. Killed for their ivory tusks, about 96 elephants a day fall victim to illegal trafficking.[20]

Around the world, endangered plants and animals are on the brink of extinction because of illegal trafficking. Although SDZG has worked on this problem for years, we realized that our new vision to end extinction demanded that we step up our efforts to fight illegal trafficking, maximizing our impact within the first year of implementing The Call.

One area was SDZG's involvement with CITES. "SDZG developed a CITES subcommittee to participate in the discussions contributing to the implementation of CITES around the globe," explained Suzanne. In October 2016, our subcommittee attended the CITES gathering, called the Conference of the Parties (COP). "We are now better positioned to lend our voice to important discussions about trade in endangered species," she said. "Illegal trade is a serious conservation threat to a significant proportion of endangered or threatened species, so this effort is squarely aligned with The Call." Our work with CITES also allowed SDZG to leverage our relationship with the Association of Zoos and Aquariums (AZA) to support and enhance the work of zoos everywhere.

We raised awareness locally as well. In October 2016, SDZG hosted 45 technology specialists for a three-day Zoohackathon. In this event, created in partnership with the US Department of State, wildlife experts posed real-life trafficking problems to programmers and coders who developed and presented usable solutions. At the end of the event, project winners were chosen. One group from San Diego, Wild Track, is developing its product to help route live information about poaching events in the wild to anti-poaching patrols. Another team came up with Safe Souvenirs, a smartphone app that helps travelers avoid unwittingly purchasing trafficked items that harm wildlife populations.

Five other zoos around the world hosted Zoohackathons during the same 48-hour period. "The event was an opportunity for the San Diego tech community to come together to address wildlife trafficking with creative technological solutions in a compressed time frame," Suzanne reported. "SDZG staff stayed on-site to facilitate the event and provide the support needed to inform the participants about the scope of wildlife trafficking."

The Zoohackathon opportunity gave SDZG the means to build a stronger relationship with the US Department of State. It further demonstrated our commitment to highlighting and addressing the significant conservation threat from wildlife trafficking. "It also brought into that fight a community of highly innovative individuals from San Diego that had not yet been tapped for addressing this problem," Suzanne noted. "It broadened our support base in our own backyard and enabled us to have a stronger impact in addressing the illegal wildlife trade."

Wildlife Trafficking Research and Collaboration

In addition to fighting illegal wildlife trafficking, we expanded our work to understand the drivers of the trade. We built many flourishing partnerships around the world, including several in Southeast Asia, where the use of bear parts and bear bile is a major trafficking problem in some countries. This cruel industry collects bile from the gallbladders of living bears by inserting metal collection tubes into perpetually open wounds in the bears. In Lao People's Democratic Republic (PDR), years of effort had failed to curb the practice, so SDZG worked with many in-country partners and local authorities to get to the source of the problem. We studied the reasons people use the products, the cultural significance, and possible substitutes. We were able to find out what local people knew about wildlife and their attitudes about the animals and plants in their environment.

One of the leaders of the project was David O'Connor, a researcher in the SDZG global partnerships division. "What began as an effort to understand why people in Lao PDR purchase bear bile and other bear parts," David recalled, "has now become an effort to understand the attitudes, beliefs, and other drivers that underpin the use of illegal wildlife products from a number of species in countries throughout Southeast Asia and China." Results from our research with in-country partners will help inform targeted demand-reduction campaigns and other efforts that resonate with consumers. We now have systems in place to track the impact of these campaigns and determine whether we have been successful in reducing the market for bear parts as a component of addressing wildlife trafficking worldwide. "It exemplifies both our collaborative, locally led approach and our commitment to use research results rather than opinions to solve conservation problems," David explained. "Our expanding network of partners increases impact and streamlines our efforts. It helps to ensure coordination among the collaborators so that no one is duplicating work."

Solid Financial Health

One concern we often heard during The Lynx years was that a conservation mission would harm SDZG's financial health. Financial fitness remains vital to ensuring the long-term viability of our organization and our ability to fund the initiatives crucial to the success of The Call.

With careful planning, we were able to make it work: from a financial standpoint, SDZG has grown by leaps and bounds. Our revenue, for instance, was at $136 million in 2001 as we began work on our first vision and our Lynx strategic plans. By 2017, nearly two years after implementing The Call, our revenue stood at $346 million.

A key financial indicator for SDZG is unrestricted operating income, which indicates the amount of money coming in that is not designated for a specific purpose. As a nonprofit, we receive many donations or bequests that are designated for a specific purpose or program—so they can't be used for shoring up the organization in an "unrestricted" manner. It's critical to have unrestricted income to grow the organization. "In 2001, our unrestricted operating income was negative $11 million, which was clearly unsustainable," recalled David Page, corporate director of finance. "So during The Lynx years, we focused on building out much-needed financial tools and infrastructure. The combination of executive-level vision and strategy with sophisticated financial tools resulted in a strong financial discipline. This ongoing strategic planning and decision-making continued to gain strength in 2015 with the advent of The Call." By 2017, we had a positive $28 million in unrestricted operating income—an improvement of $39 million.

We thoroughly examined our funding model to ensure our work to end extinction aligned with the work we did at the Zoo and the Safari Park. For example, for the Zoo's Conrad Prebys Australian Outback, we supported Australian animals in our care with a fundraising campaign—but we also added $500,000 above construction costs to support a study on the genetics of Tasmanian devil facial tumor disease in the wild. We continued this with the next major construction project, the Tull Family Tiger Trail at the Safari Park, adding $500,000 to our fundraising goal to conduct an island-wide survey of tiger camera-trap data on Sumatra. And with the Zoo's Conrad Prebys Africa Rocks, we raised an extra $500,000 to fund a study that looked at the habitats for red ruffed lemurs in Madagascar.

Of course, there is still much to be done. The first phase of The Call will be completed within a few years, but the vision to "lead the fight against extinction" will take much longer to realize. In the meantime, SDZG will continue to work to save species, to engage collaborators—and to find new ways to deliver on this dream and measure our progress.

"We cannot do it alone," observed Dr. Fred Frye, former SDZG board chair and trustee emeritus. "It will take physical and political will to accomplish this daunting task. As a board member and native San Diegan, I have been involved with the Zoo from a very young age. We do have an opportunity to make a difference. I am confident that our call to end extinction will be heard and that we will be successful."

Rick Gulley, who chaired the board during the creation of The Call, referenced the classic psychological theory Maslow's hierarchy of needs: "We've moved from the bottom of the pyramid, where we are just providing food to the animals," he said. "We're now making a conscious decision to focus on conservation."

At SDZG, we know we have a responsibility to do more. Rick explained, "If we're not going to do it, who will? We have the scope and size and the benefits that have been given to us, in addition to the skilled leadership and management here. We could sit on our financial reserves and use the excess money to build bigger structures, but we've chosen a higher path."

Kea Spurrier, SDZG's capital campaign director and associate development director, who helped develop The Call's operational plan, said that it helped her to think more strategically. "We want to become a conservation organization that has two great zoos, not just a zoo that does conservation, and I think The Call is taking us to the next level." She noted that this vision would not have been possible 10 years ago, when SDZG first tried to become a conservation organization: "We've flipped our mission and vision, putting conservation on top. We're clear now on where we need to go to help plants and animals have a long-lasting future."

Northern White Rhinos: A Symbol of Change

No story better exemplifies The Call than the plight of the northern white rhinoceros. Consistent with its vision to lead the fight against extinction, SDZG made an organization-wide commitment to rescue the northern white rhino from the brink of extinction. As of 2018, there are only two left in the world, and those that remain are now old females. Therefore, natural solutions will

What Is Your "Nola"?

Nola and the predicament of her fellow northern white rhinos became a symbol for change at SDZG. Many other stories exemplify our conservation work, but the story of Nola and her subspecies became very personal for us—both before and after she passed away. It exemplified our mission of saving species worldwide (white rhinos) by uniting our expertise in animal care (of Nola) and conservation science (efforts to save the northern white rhino subspecies) with our dedication to inspiring passion for nature (the reasons to care about rhinos).

Nola, who is represented on the cover of this book, has come to symbolize the meaning of The Call for our staff, board members, and volunteers. What is the symbol of change in your own organization? What key challenge or success serves as an emblem for the difference you want to make in the world?

not be enough to save this important subspecies. The project is a symbol of The Call, pushing SDZG to envision new types of scientific solutions, new ways to collaborate with partners, and new ways to engage the public in its cause.

SDZG cared for several of the remaining northern white rhinos for 30 years. In November 2015, Nola, the third remaining northern white rhino, passed away peacefully at the Safari Park. "We were honored to care for her at the end of her life," said Jane Kennedy, lead keeper at the Safari Park. A heartfelt outpouring of sympathy and condolences followed Nola's passing as people around the world paid tribute to the rhino that had impressed and inspired so many during her lifetime.

Nola was not only a much-loved individual in her own right—she was also a symbol of the extinction crisis facing rhinos around the world. "Since the loss of our own Nola the rhino, our outstanding Zoo family has embarked on the amazing rhino rescue project," said Sandra Brue, a SDZG board member. "One can just see and feel the excitement, commitment, passion, and positive momentum amp up and spread throughout the entire organization. San Diego Zoo Global doesn't just have a mission statement. We are wildlife conservation missionaries, and this is now our life's purpose."

San Diego Zoo Global is fully committed to saving rhinos from extinction. Through collaborative, science-based, multidisciplinary conservation efforts at the Safari Park, we have successfully added the births of more than 90 southern white rhinos, nearly 70 greater one-horned rhinos, and more than a dozen black rhinos to the worldwide population. In addition, the San Diego Zoo Institute for Conservation Research is preserving living cell lines from as many rhinos as possible, including northern white rhinos.

"The initiative to save the last of the northern white rhinos fits into The Call so well that these animals have become the symbol of our battle cry," said Dr. Don Janssen, retired corporate director of animal health for SDZG. "We've taken on this type of challenge before, with loggerhead shrikes and California condors, for instance. The work needed to save those species was seemingly impossible. Now, with The Call in place, it has allowed our staff to worry less about how to prioritize the many things we could be doing, because we have focus." Don observed that the northern white rhino project has excited people throughout the organization: "We had been preparing for years for this opportunity, and now The Call has allowed us to converge to help these rhinos."

A Story That Belongs to Everyone

The story of the plight of the rhinos resonates across SDZG.

Our keepers, veterinarians, nutritionists, and specialists at the San Diego Zoo and the San Diego Zoo Safari Park are dedicated to providing the best care possible for the rhinos—and every animal—in their care. Whether they care for rhinos directly or not, they see rhinos as an iconic representative of their stewardship of all animals. Our scientists, technicians, and others from the San Diego Zoo Institute for Conservation Research focus on species-wide efforts, both in San Diego and in the rhinos' home ranges. Whether their projects involve rhinos or not, they know that the rhino rescue initiative symbolizes the new frontiers of science that will be explored for endangered species. And our employees who do not work directly with animals and plants can see that they are helping our organization to thrive so that SDZG can ultimately do more to help rhinos and other species.

At SDZG, we stand for rhinos. We stand for giant pandas, cycads, coastal cactus wrens, Caribbean iguanas, and hundreds of other rare animal and plant species. Whether the representatives of these species are in human care or in the wild, we believe that we can facilitate long-term conservation efforts to help these species. It's daunting to think about ending extinction, but endangered species of plants and animals are now at a critical juncture. We believe that it is our destiny to unite with collaborators and do what we can to save species.

Our battle cry: "End extinction!"

We'd love to hear about your successes, your own best practices, and your challenges with strategic planning and management. Drop us a line at thecall@sandiegozoo.org.

EPILOGUE

*"The arrogance of success is to think that what you did yesterday
will be sufficient for tomorrow."*
William Pollard, physicist

At San Diego Zoo Global, our conservation work has become more focused with time. We moved from having scientists and curators working on any project they chose to a prioritization method that emphasized mission relevance, impact, and inter- and intraorganizational collaboration. Then, with the advent of The Call, we added another layer of criteria, asking ourselves, "In which conservation arenas are we most suited to lead the fight?"

The result led to SDZG choosing to laser in on 10 major conservation initiatives. Although we continue to work on many other wildlife conservation issues, the following initiatives will receive the highest commitment of resources and focus from our organization:

- **San Diego End Extinction**—saving flagship southwestern species such as Torrey pines, bighorn sheep, and burrowing owls
- **Saving African Primates**—preserving primates such as chimpanzees, gorillas, and lemurs
- **Bears of the World**—helping species like Andean bears, giant pandas, and sloth bears
- **Kenya Conservation**—working with local communities to conserve species like African elephants, rhinos, giraffes, and vultures
- **Island Conservation**—conserving island species such as Tasmanian devils, Caribbean rock iguanas, and Lord Howe Island stick insects
- **Andes to Amazon**—preserving iconic species like the giant otter, jaguar, and Andean condor
- **Frozen Zoo Global Expansion**—biobanking critically endangered

species such as Asian turtles, California condors, and native California plants

- **Genetic Rescue**—preventing extinction of the northern white rhino, black-footed ferret, and other species
- **Climate Change**—focusing on the most highly impacted species like polar bears, koalas, African penguins, and many plants
- **Wildlife Trafficking**—benefiting illegally trafficked animals and plants, including Asian elephants, orchids, rhinoceroses, and tigers

We are certainly not going to do this alone. Each of these 10 initiatives has a lengthy list of major conservation collaborators—more than 100 in all.

Banking on Conservation

For four decades, SDZG scientists have been collecting genetic material from animals and plants—including ova, sperm, DNA, seeds, and living cell lines. Samples are taken as part of routine medical procedures and frozen for safe-keeping. As of 2018, genetic material from more than 10,000 individual animals, representing over 1,000 animal species and subspecies, have been banked in the Frozen Zoo. Thus far, they have been used for countless genetic and reproductive science efforts, including genome-sequencing projects for African elephants, two-toed sloths, and gorillas, and assisted reproduction of birds and mammals—with many more species to come. SDZG also has a flourishing seed bank where we house hundreds of seed collections from various rare and endangered plant species.

In the Frozen Zoo, we are working with our partners to:

- Develop "barcodes" as a reference that will allow authorities to determine if bushmeat is from an endangered species, as well as the location from which the sample originated
- Guide the reintroduction efforts for the critically endangered Przewalski's

horse by comparing the genetic makeup between samples in the Frozen Zoo and ancient DNA samples extracted from museum skins

- Participate in the Genome 10K project—a global initiative to sequence the genomes of 10,000 species—to become better stewards of the world's wildlife

In the future, we hope to facilitate the formation of a collaborative network of cryobanks under the umbrella of a global wildlife biobank. This network would be crucial to helping to save plant and animal species.

Scientific Solutions

There may be only a couple of northern white rhinos on the planet, but don't count them out yet. SDZG has made a commitment that this subspecies will not blink out on our watch, and we're doing everything we can to see them restored. On the horizon, we hope to provide a scientific solution. There are cells from 12 of these beautiful rhinos in the Frozen Zoo, representing a significant amount of genetic diversity. Working with our partners, we have successfully cultivated stem cells from these rhino samples and one day hope to create a northern white rhino embryo to be implanted in a southern white rhino female. This female would serve as a surrogate mother at our Nikita Kahn Rhino Rescue Center.

"The most incredible part of this genetic rescue technology is that, once it is accomplished, it could be adapted for Javan rhinos, Sumatran rhinos, or even species other than rhinos," noted Dr. Allison Alberts, SDZG chief conservation and research officer. "It has the potential to truly be a game-changer for species teetering on the brink of extinction."

Kenya: A Model for Collaboration

The Call requires us to pick our battles, to lead the charge, and to sustain the momentum. For example, Kenya is home to many species of endangered animals and plants, and we are using the country as a testing ground for collaborative action that will help lions, giraffes, elephants, leopards, rhinos, zebras, vultures, and a critically endangered antelope called the hirola. This expanded approach to collaboration not only helps the animals but also helps the people of Kenya, who are a vital element of a strong in-country community conservation effort. We collaborate on projects to provide peace and security programs that thwart poachers and engage local youth, as well as wildlife and forestry management programs. Together with our partners, we also help with enterprise projects, which address tourism and microenterprises, and infrastructure and equipment such as vehicles, outposts, roads, and wells. This integrated approach involves more than 10 SDZG departments and nearly 20 international and in-country partners.

To achieve the full-spectrum conservation model outlined in The Call, we must serve as the facilitators to harness the expertise of everyone involved. We bring a track record in conservation science, animal care, and veterinary service to the table—but we must partner with others who have in-country expertise, land management know-how, and other key elements that are outside of our conservation niche. We are working to align the endeavors of all concerned and make plans for the future—laying the groundwork now for what we hope will evolve into a template for future collaborations.

The Call, however, is about more than just our conservation efforts around the world. It requires that every employee and volunteer in San Diego also be aligned with our mission to end extinction—whether they are helping to create a television commercial about conservation, preparing food for the elephants at the Zoo or the Safari Park, stocking educational books in the gift shop, or driving a tour bus and relaying stories about endangered species.

The Call has solidly aligned our goals, helping SDZG's thousands of staff members and volunteers to truly make a difference in the global effort to save animals and plants from extinction.

NOTES

1. WWF, *Living Planet Report 2014: Species and Spaces, People and Places*, ed. Richard McLellan et al., 2014, assets.worldwildlife.org/publications/723/files/original/WWF-LPR2014-low_res.pdf.

2. "IUCN Red List of Threatened Species," IUCN, iucnredlist.org.

3. Michael G. Barbour, et al., *California's Changing Landscapes: Diversity and Conservation of California Vegetation* (Sacramento: California Native Plant Society, 1993).

4. Rodolfo Dirzo et al., "Defaunation in the Anthropocene," *Science* 345, no. 6195 (July 25, 2014): 401–406.

5. Michael R. W. Rands et al., "Biodiversity Conservation: Challenges beyond 2010," *Science* 329, no. 5997 (September 10, 2010): 1298–1303.

6. "Legal Wildlife Trade," wildlife trade monitoring, TRAFFIC, traffic.org/trade.

7. Candee Wilde, "Evaluating the Endangered Species Act: Trends in Mega-Petitions, Judicial Review, and Budget Constraints Reveal a Costly Dilemma for Species Conservation," *Villanova Environmental Law Journal* 25, no. 1 (2014): 307–350.

8. C. M. Lees and J. Wilcken, "Sustaining the Ark: The Challenges Faced by Zoos in Maintaining Viable Populations," *International Zoo Yearbook* 43, no. 1 (January 2009): 6–18.

9. Daniel F. Doak et al., "What Is the Future of Conservation?" *Trends in Ecology & Evolution* 29, no. 2 (February 2014): 77–81.

10 Jacob S. Sherkow and Henry T. Greely, "What if Extinction Is Not Forever?" *Science* 340, no. 6128 (April 5, 2013): 32–33.

11. American Alliance of Museums, *The Reinvention of AAM: A Case Study*, 2009, museumalliance.org/docs/default-source/about-us/the-reinvention-of-aam-a-case-study.pdf.

12. Simon Sinek, *Start with Why: How Great Leaders Inspire Everyone to Take Action* (New York: Portfolio/Penguin, 2011).

13. Simone Joyaux, "Unraveling Development: What Is Donor-Centrism?" *Nonprofit Quarterly*, June 18, 2009, nonprofitquarterly.org/2009/06/18/unraveling-development-what-is-donor-centrism/.

14. Orit Gadiesh and James L. Gilbert, "Transforming Corner-Office Strategy into Frontline Action," *Harvard Business Review* 79, no. 5 (May 2001): 73–79.

15. William Calvin, *How Brains Think: Evolving Intelligence, Then and Now* (London: Weidenfeld & Nicolson, 1997).

16. Jim Collins, *Good to Great: Why Some Companies Make the Leap . . . and Others Don't* (New York: HarperBusiness, 2001).

17. Richard Chait, William P. Ryan, and Barbara E. Taylor, *Governance as Leadership: Reframing the Work of Nonprofit Boards* (Hoboken, NJ: John Wiley & Sons, 2005).

18. Jim Collins, *Good to Great and the Social Sectors: Why Business Thinking Is Not the Answer; A Monograph to Accompany Good to Great* (self-pub., 2005).

19. David Hancocks, *A Different Nature: The Paradoxical World of Zoos and Their Uncertain Future* (Berkeley: University of California Press, 2001).

20. "96 Elephants," Wildlife Conservation Society, wcs.org/96-elephants.

APPENDIX A

The Call
San Diego Zoo Global Strategic Plan, 2015

Note: This is the plan approved by the SDZG board and executive staff in 2015 and used to implement the changes detailed in the book. It is included here as a reference to describe the needs and priorities that went into making The Call. The numbers of species and other information have changed since 2015.

This plan is a call to action: to awaken the world to the plight of wildlife— and to provide hope for the future of nature.

Our Philosophy

San Diego Zoo Global represents nearly a century of work on behalf of wildlife, but the state of wildlife is now at a critical juncture. San Diego Zoo Global is uniquely positioned to lead the fight against wildlife extinction.

Why us? Why now? San Diego Zoo Global is financially strong and operates two world-renowned zoos as well as a proven conservation effort. So, why choose such an audacious vision? Because species are disappearing faster than ever and stemming the tide of extinction will take enormous creativity, resources, and focus. Despite our decades-long commitment to conservation, animal and plant species continue to vanish at record speeds.

We are at a crossroads. We can choose to continue on our current path. San Diego Zoo Global has a great track record of operational excellence and wildlife conservation results. But our research shows that we are the best organization to serve as a catalyst amongst our peers and partners by taking on a new role in the global community. Our external review shows that there is hope for saving species on a grand scale in the coming decade, but not without a transformational shift in our priorities and a sea change in our approach.

We must earn a leadership role. Delivering on our vision won't be easy. It will require a plan that challenges the status quo and forces us to admit that we can no longer continue along our current trajectory. Leading this fight against extinction can only be earned through sustained focus, an unflinching look at our organization, and a willingness to take bold steps to adapt.

We can't succeed alone. Achieving our vision will be impossible without key collaboration with others who have complementary areas of expertise. San Diego Zoo Global will have to conduct itself in a highly professional, nimble, and innovative manner. We will have to seize the public's attention, energize people, and appeal to the media . . . because these practices will become the engines of our message and its execution.

We need to develop ways to radically slow the rate of species decline. If we truly want to lead the fight against extinction, we need to recognize both the magnitude and timeline of what will be required to do so. Then we will develop collaborative strategies in many fields to address this emergency.

We are ready for the challenge. We are eager to get started on the road to our new vision. This will be a long, tough, complicated challenge that will require a multifaceted approach to achieve transformational results. At San Diego Zoo Global, though, we aren't going to settle for anything less.

Mission

The purpose of our organization

San Diego Zoo Global is committed to saving species worldwide by uniting our expertise in animal care and conservation science with our dedication to inspiring passion for nature.

Values

The core tenets of our culture

THE ROAR

1. Make a difference for wildlife.
2. Share the wonder of nature.
3. Feel the passion for what we do.
4. Breed financial stability.
5. Succeed together.
6. Remember the roar . . . and pass it on.

Vision

Our chosen future

Our vision is to lead the fight against extinction.

Strategic Priorities

Crucial elements to bring our vision to life

To lead the fight against extinction, San Diego Zoo Global will need to:

- UNITE, internally and externally, with a laser focus on our cause.
- FIGHT against extinction of animal and plant species.
- IGNITE a life-changing passion for wildlife.

Strategies to lead the fight against extinction

UNITE

Goal: Focus on stemming the tide of species extinction by rallying our internal stakeholders around our vision and building a mighty league of external collaborators.

Strategies to UNITE

1. BUILD CAPACITY

   Focus internally and externally on organizational capacity building: select critical collaborators whose strengths increase our reach and boost the bench strength of our staff, board, and volunteers.

2. MAXIMIZE OUR RESOURCES

   Ensure that we have the financial capacity and fiscal responsibility to become the most effective wildlife conservation organization in the world . . . both now and in the future.

FIGHT

Goal: Fight extinction with an integrated conservation approach that includes both the species in our care as well as animals and plants in the wild.

Strategies to FIGHT

1. PICK OUR BATTLES

   As much as we want to, we can't save every species, and we can't do it alone. We will prioritize and focus our work on the species that are the best fit for our niche.

2. LEAD THE CHARGE

   Enhance our emphasis on full-spectrum conservation, applying leading-edge scientific methods and husbandry solutions to our priority species.

3. SUSTAIN THE MOMENTUM

   Collaborate with others who can maintain our conservation efforts as long as necessary.

IGNITE

Goal: Awaken a global audience to take personal responsibility for the future of wildlife.

Strategies to IGNITE

1. IGNITE PASSION

   Spark an obsession for saving wildlife.

2. RECRUIT CHAMPIONS

   Use grand gestures and unique methods to attract advocates to our cause.

3. INSPIRE PERSONAL RESPONSIBILITY

   Provide people with a new way of life—specific individual actions that we each must take in order to make a change in the wildlife conservation landscape.

EVIDENCE

Results of an internal and external environmental scan that led to the formation of The Call

How San Diego Zoo Global is uniquely suited to achieve this bold vision:

Wildlife is in trouble

When it comes to wildlife conservation, our key message is one of hope—an optimistic expectation that we will be able to do what needs to be done to help stem the tide of extinction for key species. However, despite our decades-long commitment to conservation, animal and plant species continue to vanish at record speeds, and it is impossible to ignore the facts that underpin the plight of wildlife. Just a few of the crucial data points that demonstrate a need to shift our emphasis from a "zoo that does conservation" to a "conservation zoo" are listed below:

- Population sizes of vertebrate species have decreased worldwide by more than 50 percent since 1970.
- Forty-one percent of amphibian species are listed as threatened or extinct in the wild.
- In our own backyard, Southern California remains one of the world's biodiversity hotspots, with a high proportion of critically endangered species.
- One in five plant species is threatened with extinction.
- The loss of species around the world doesn't just impact wildlife, it causes disruptions in pollination, natural pest control, nutrient cycling, water quality, and human health.
- From an economic standpoint, the value of losing biodiverse ecosystems is estimated to be 10 to 100 times the cost of maintaining them.

Résumé for the position of Ending Extinction

PROFILE

San Diego Zoo Global is uniquely qualified to fill the position of Ending Extinction. Our core strength is in the thousands of people over the course of 100 years who have built a credible knowledge base and history of caring for the most rare and endangered plants and animals on the planet. We are collaborative, innovative, and hopeful—all key attributes for succeeding in the position.

Skills

LEADERSHIP

We've been the first for many things, such as housing rare animals for the first time in the United States and having the first of many species born at a zoo. But leadership is not about doing things first, it's in teaching others how to replicate our first-time successes. It's also in collaborating with global partners to further mutual goals.

COMMUNICATION

We reach tens of millions of people each year, either through media or by visitation to one of our parks. Each person we reach is someone who can make a choice to support ending extinction. Our communication style is factual and hopeful, with the intent to inspire people to positive action.

SCIENCE

Our knowledge and application of natural sciences is second to none. We are the ones people come to when they need expertise for saving critically endangered species. We are training the next generation of conservationists.

Experience

Koala breeding and conservation   **1925–present**

San Diego Zoo Global was the first to host koalas outside of Australia, starting in 1925. In 1960, we were the first to breed them in the United States. Today, we not only manage the largest colony outside of Australia, we also provide research support to koala conservation projects in the wild.

California condor recovery   **1982–present**

A bird that was nearly extinct in the wild is now flying again in its native range, thanks to the expertise of San Diego Zoo Global and its collaboration with many partners. Once considered an impossible project, the California condor program has not only been successful, it has become a model for other bird conservation programs worldwide.

References

Hundreds of additional examples available upon request.

EVIDENCE

San Diego Zoo Global can make a difference

What can we achieve for species conservation when we pick our battles, lead the charge, and sustain our momentum? We will abandon the idea that we can do it all alone and focus on recruiting like-minded partners to join us in our cause.

Conservation results

Here are a few key metrics and results that demonstrate the scope of our work and reference the power of recruiting champions to join us in the fight against extinction:

- Currently, more than 230 at-risk species (IUCN or USFWS-listed) are the focus of active SDZG conservation work.
- Of these, 48 species were successfully bred at the San Diego Zoo and the San Diego Zoo Safari Park in 2014.
- SDZG conservation projects highlighted 143 of these species.
- In 2014, SDZG carried out or supported conservation work in 76 countries worldwide, in collaboration with more than 250 partner organizations.

Collaborative reintroduction programs

Key species reintroduction programs that demonstrate collaborative conservation success:

- Addax: 14 partners
- Andean condor: 6 partners
- Anegada iguana: 6 partners
- California condor: 8 partners
- Desert tortoise: 3 partners
- Guam rail: 3 partners
- Indian rhino: 6 partners

- Light-footed clapper rail: 9 partners
- Mountain yellow-legged frog: 6 partners
- Nene: 8 partners
- Pacific pocket mouse: 3 partners
- Peninsular pronghorn: 8 partners
- Przewalski's horse: 4 partners
- Puaiohi: 8 partners
- Saiga: 5 partners
- San Clemente loggerhead shrike: 4 partners
- Scimitar-horned oryx: 13 partners
- Southern ground hornbill: 6 partners
- Stephen's kangaroo rat: 5 partners
- Tasmanian devil: 4 partners
- Turks and Caicos iguana: 6 partners

EVIDENCE

How we will achieve exponential results with the right partners and policies

Here are just a few examples of external trends that highlight opportunities for SDZG to engage in key collaborative relationships:

- The Endangered Species Act (ESA)—the cornerstone of species conservation in our country—is under threat. We have the opportunity to work with partners to advocate for legislation that provides the strongest protection for species and supports our vision of ending extinction.
- The illegal wildlife trade is becoming more profitable, with an estimated value of billions of dollars annually. We are being invited to join forces with the US State Department, USFWS law enforcement, and USAID, which are leading efforts to combat wildlife trade.

- The Association of Zoos and Aquariums (AZA) is launching a new "SAFE" initiative to save at least 100 species, in which we will be a key participant.
- There is insufficient space in zoos to hold, let alone breed, the number of endangered species that would benefit from such programs. The Alliance for Sustainable Wildlife serves as a model for how zoos can collaborate to increase the resources available to support assurance populations and reintroduction programs.
- World Wildlife Fund (WWF), World Conservation Society (WCS), and Conservation International (CI) are de-emphasizing science in favor of ecosystem services and human use approaches. All will require science-based partners such as SDZG to effectively conserve species and manage natural resources.
- Technological advances in genomics are bringing new importance to the Frozen Zoo® and other biobanking efforts and their role in ending extinction. SDZG has the opportunity to become the hub of a global genetic rescue effort.

EVIDENCE

How The Call will impact Zoo and Safari Park visitorship and guest experience
As stewards of animal welfare, we must provide the context for people to appreciate animals and plants so that they will be motivated to take personal responsibility for changing the fate of wildlife.

Providing authentic experiences

Younger generations are growing up in constant contact with technology, creating new social norms for experiencing the world. In contrast, authentic experiences will hold a different kind of value. Our Zoo, Safari Park, and global conservation efforts will provide genuine, immersive experiences with nature and wildlife. These opportunities will be enhancements to social media, citizen science, communication, and learning for future generations. Active participation is already significant among guests and visitors as they seek authentic experiences during visits to our facilities. The demand for special experiences has increased significantly over the past several years, and future visitors will be exposed to even more new opportunities.

Showcasing our vision

New exhibits and experiences will be conceived and designed to demonstrate how we are fulfilling our vision. Each new addition will provide an opportunity to demonstrate how plants and animals are thriving in our care and returning to the wild. Following these experiences, guests will choose to support our vision through their visitation.

Engaging learners

Learning in an immersive environment will continue to be a valuable engagement for young minds seeking knowledge and active skills for understanding and working in the world around us. Their contributions and participation will be important collaborations in our efforts to secure a future in which wildlife can thrive.

Changing perceptions

The public perception of zoos is changing, along with expectations. The beliefs and values of visitors must be addressed so that zoos can continue to be seen as authentic experiences. By carefully listening to critics while continuing to demonstrate our contribution through learning, conservation, science, and social engagement, we will focus on creating opportunities for the animals and plants in our care to thrive.

Making emotional connections

Our guests are introduced to living ambassadors through on-site experiences. We will call attention to our conservation expertise while creating an emotional connection and a bond with the natural world.

EVIDENCE

Funding and metrics

To fund The Call, we will . . .

1. Maintain and enhance our existing revenue streams.
2. Create new revenue streams through:
   - Collaborations and partnerships
   - Acquisitions
   - Consulting
   - New product development
   - New service area development
3. Review and reconsider resource allocation.
4. Discontinue nonproductive programs.

Key Performance Metrics (KPMs) for success

1. Conservation impact
2. Measures of long-term financial sustainability
3. Levels of member support
4. Levels of conservation project support

Our keys to success: conservation impact, long-term support, and sustainability

WE WILL LEAD THE FIGHT AGAINST EXTINCTION

The fate of nature is at a critical juncture, and San Diego Zoo Global must adapt to this reality in its second 100 years.

This is a wake-up call: to unite people to our cause, to fight against extinction, and to ignite a life-changing passion for wildlife.

We will have to collaborate to slow the rate of species extinction. We must also provide the context for people to appreciate animals and plants so that they will be motivated to take personal responsibility for changing the fate of wildlife. Join us in the fight to END EXTINCTION!

APPENDIX B
For Further Reading

Strategic Planning

- Strategic Planning, a free two-hour online course offered by the SDZG Academy at sdzglobalacademy.org/courses
- Association for Strategic Planning at strategyassociation.org
- *Strategic and Systems Thinking* by Stephen Haines
- *Strategic Planning for Nonprofit Organizations* by Michael Allison and Jude Kaye
- *Strategy in the 21st Century* by Randall Rollinson and Earl Young
- *Good Strategy/Bad Strategy* by Richard Rumelt
- *Strategy Journeys: A Guide to Effective Strategic Planning* by David Booth
- *HBR's 10 Must Reads on Strategy* by Harvard Business Review
- *Creative Strategy Generation* by Bob Caporale
- *AHEAD: Strategy Is the Way to a Better Future* by Lee Crumbaugh
- *Crafting Effective Mission and Vision Statements* by Emil Angelica

Leadership and Governance

- *Governance as Leadership* by Richard P. Chait, William P. Ryan, and Barbara E. Taylor
- *The Ultimate Board Member's Book* by Kay Sprinkel Grace
- *The Nonprofit Leadership Team* by Fisher Howe
- *The Nonprofit Board Answer Book* by BoardSource
- *Blue Avocado: A Magazine of Nonprofits Insurance Alliance Group* at blueavocado.org

Strategic Facilitation

- *The Facilitator's Fieldbook* by Thomas Justice and David W. Jamieson
- *Extreme Facilitation* by Suzanne Ghais
- *The Facilitator's Guide to Participatory Decision-Making* by Sam Kaner
- *The Skilled Facilitator* by Roger Schwarz
- *The Executive Guide to Facilitating Strategy* by Michael Wilkinson

Environmental Scanning and Measuring Impact

- *Impact and Excellence* by Sheri Chaney Jones
- *Measure What Matters* by Katie Delahaye Paine
- *Data Driven Nonprofits* by Steve MacLaughlin
- *The Nonprofit Dashboard* by Lawrence M. Butler
- *Proactive Intelligence* by John J. McGonagle and Carolyn M. Vella
- "Finding the Unicorn" by Lynne M. Brown (on her website ibosswell.com)

Organizational Greatness and Sustainability

- *Good to Great* by Jim Collins
- *Good to Great and the Social Sectors* by Jim Collins
- *Business Model Generation* by Alexander Osterwalder and Yves Pigneur
- *Forces for Good* by Leslie R. Crutchfield and Heather McLeod Grant
- *Nonprofit Sustainability* by Jeanne Bell and Jan Masaoka
- *Find Your Why*, a book and an amazing TED talk by Simon Sinek: ted.com/talks/simon_sinek_how_great_leaders_inspire_action

Living Your Strategic Plan: Execution and Change Management

- *The Art of Relevance* by Nina Simon
- *Strategic Project Management Made Simple* by Terry Schmidt
- *The Change Monster* by Jeanie Daniel Duck
- *Operating Model Canvas* by Andrew Campbell, Mikel Gutierrez, and Mark Lancelott
- *Becoming Strategic* by Timi Gleason
- *Managing Change and Transition* by Harvard Business Essentials
- *Free-Range Thinking*, a free newsletter available on Andy Goodman's website at thegoodmancenter.com

APPENDIX C
Glossary of Terms Used in This Book

You will find planning terms defined differently in every business book you read. This glossary explains the definitions as they are used by San Diego Zoo Global (SDZG). It also includes many of the conservation-related and SDZG-specific abbreviations used in this book.

Assurance population: Group of animals or plants relocated to a secondary location as a backup population to serve as a safety net and ensure that genetic diversity is preserved.

AZA: Abbreviation for the Association of Zoos and Aquariums, a nonprofit organization dedicated to the advancement of zoos and aquariums in the areas of conservation, education, science, and recreation.

Big ideas (see **strategic priorities**)

Capacity building: Work that develops and strengthens the long-term viability of an organization, association, project, individual, or community.

Charter: Document that specifies the responsibilities, scope, and other details of a group's work.

CITES: Convention on International Trade in Endangered Species of Wild Fauna and Flora, which is an agreement between governments to ensure that international trade of wild animals and plants does not threaten species survival.

Environmental scan: Broad assessment of the factors that may affect your organization, both now and in the foreseeable future.

Ex situ: Outside of a species' natural geographic range; as with a translocation or a managed care setting (such as a zoo, sanctuary, and so on).

Execution: Putting a plan into action; also known as **implementation**.

Facilitative process: Moving forward by bringing stakeholders together.

Facilitator: Professional with no "skin in the game" who helps a group to achieve its goals through best practices, agenda development, and guided discussions.

Fiduciary: Overseeing the resources of an organization.

Generative: Thinking that focuses on the meaning behind the knowledge, information, and data. It is about framing problems and making sense of issues on the path toward generating new ideas, as opposed to decision-making.

Goal: Result or achievement toward which effort is directed (see also **strategic priorities**).

Governance: Governing of an entity by providing oversight, ensuring that the organization delivers on its mission and that it remains financially viable.

KPI: Abbreviation for a Key Performance Indicator (also known as a Key Performance Metric). While many measurements can be used to identify movement from point A to point B, KPIs are agreed-upon metrics that are most reflective of progress toward stated goals.

ICR: Abbreviation for the Institute for Conservation Research, which is SDZG's scientific arm.

Implementation: Putting a strategic plan into action; also called **execution**.

In situ: Natural, original geographic range of a species of animals or plants.

Initiative: Significant undertaking; a major task or project.

Make The Call canvas: Prioritization tool used at SDZG to help employees and their supervisors align their actions with The Call.

Mission: Organization's purpose; its reason for existing.

Mission creep or **mission drift:** Gradually beginning to implement initiatives outside the scope of an organization's mission.

New Perspectives Strategic Planning (NPSP) team: Multidisciplinary work group at SDZG designed to evoke fresh ideas from employees who are not typically involved in strategic planning.

Objective: Goal to which effort is directed (see also **strategic priorities**).

Operational plan: Outline of the actions (or **tactics**) that will be needed to implement a strategic plan.

Opportunity cost: Benefit lost by choosing one alternative over another.

Profitable distraction: Potential initiative that will yield funding or please a donor but does not further progress toward an organization's vision. Colloquially known as a **shiny object**.

Quick win: Tactic that yields a fast result and can serve as an indicator that a plan has taken root.

RACI: A matrix of roles that assigns accountability and inclusion levels for various group members as Responsible, Accountable, Consulted, or Informed.

ROI: Return On Investment. This common term refers to the gain or loss generated from an amount of money invested.

ROM: Return On Mission/Vision. In the same way that ROI measures Return On Investment, ROM helps an organization to weigh progress that delivers on its mission and vision.

SDZG: Abbreviation for San Diego Zoo Global, the parent company of the San Diego Zoo, the San Diego Zoo Safari Park, and the San Diego Zoo Institute for Conservation Research.

Shiny object: See **profitable distraction**.

SMART: An acronym for Specific, Measurable, Achievable, Realistic, and Timebound. These are the components used to write goals and tactics.

Strategic: High-level organizational direction focused on getting from the present state to a desired future state; something that affects the nature or purpose of an organization.

Strategies: How an organization will bring its vision to life.

Strategic plan: High-level road map to get from an organization's current state to achieving its vision. The best strategic plans serve as the memorable, distilled expression of shared organizational goals.

Strategic priorities: What an organization will focus on to bring its vision to life. Also known as big ideas, major objectives, or Big Hairy Audacious Goals (BHAGs).

SWOT analysis: Abbreviation for an assessment of the internal Strengths and Weaknesses of an organization or association, overlaid with its external Opportunities and Threats.

Tactics: Measurable steps to achieve a specific strategy; tactics are found in an operational plan.

The Call: New breed of SDZG strategic plan, adopted in 2015.

The Lynx: Series of strategic plans for SDZG, completed from 2002–12.

Values: Immutable tenets that identify what an organization stands for.

Value proposition: Unique worth that an organization brings to its customers.

Vision: An organization's chosen view of the future.

Wildlife trafficking: Illegal collection, transport, and/or sale of plants and animals, alive or dead, and their parts.

ACKNOWLEDGMENTS

I worked at San Diego Zoo Global (SDZG) during the years of The Call and its predecessor, The Lynx. For most of that time, I led the Vision, Innovation, and Strategy group (VIS). This gave my VIS colleagues (Robin Keith, Peggy Blessing, and Tricia Campanella) and me a front-row seat for the key changes and tough choices that went into the making of The Call. We know firsthand how revolutionary this plan was for SDZG and for plants and animals around the world—but also how difficult and uncomfortable many of the stages were for all involved.

We would like to recognize the person who did more than anyone to make The Call possible: SDZG's CEO Doug Myers. Doug will cringe when he reads this because his style of shared leadership is at the core of this plan's success. While it is important for a CEO to have buy-in for a strategic plan, it is rare for a leader to insist on sharing the credit for the resulting accomplishments. The beauty of The Call is that it is owned by *everyone* at SDZG. Doug's humility, loyalty, and leadership fostered a culture that encouraged transformational change.

We would also like to acknowledge those who helped this book come to life, including the many people who permitted us to tell their stories here. It is hard to allow your work to be distilled to a couple of paragraphs, particularly if it represents a struggle, but everyone—whether an employee, board member, volunteer, or collaborator—was very generous with both their time and their anecdotes.

As the book was hatching, it received around-the-clock care and vast improvement from a dedicated editorial team. Georgeanne Irvine provided oversight from San Diego Zoo Global Press, calling on her decades of experience with SDZG and her expertise as an author of many of her own books.

Betsy Holt, publisher of Beckon Books, made this book readable and kept its author sane. Artist Lori Sandstrom created the amazing cover for this book as a tribute to Nola, as well as the lovely charts and graphics. Vicky Shea is responsible for the overall look of the book, which is greatly enhanced by her attention to detail. Dr. Mary Sekulovich, one of the world's best editors and an amazing historian of SDZG lore, was instrumental in helping the book through its early stages. There were many others on the editorial team at Southwestern Publishing Group who came together to complete this book, and it was immensely improved by the entire team effort.

We'd like to thank the many thought partners and change agents who have given advice or acted as a sounding board over the years, as their input greatly enhanced the resulting plans and leadership that informed The Call. At the top of this list are Peg Harvey-Sweeney, Dr. Bob Wiese, Dr. Allison Alberts, Mark Stuart, Dr. Bruce Rideout, Judy Kinsell, Steve Tappan, Dwight Scott, Wendy Bulger, Marge Sheldon, Bob McClure, Dr. Linda Lowenstine, Dr. Don Janssen, Dr. Nadine Lamberski, Cliff Hague, Ted Molter, Shawn Dixon, Javade Chaudhri, Yvonne Larsen, Dr. Fred Frye, Berit Durler, Robert Horsman, Suzanne Hall, Mick Musella, Paula Brock, Becky Lynn, Rick Gulley, David Page, Tammy Rach, Victoria Garrison, and Judi Myers. They are joined by a pool of people too numerous to mention but whose willingness to "trust the process" has made a world of difference. Thanks to everyone for the reality checks, sage advice, and the gift of feedback!

Finally, I would personally like to acknowledge the incredible VIS team. Few people are aware of the detailed planning, artful facilitation, and extensive project management it takes to keep SDZG and many of our collaborators focused on the fight against extinction.

—Beth Branning

ABOUT SAN DIEGO ZOO GLOBAL

San Diego Zoo Global (SDZG) is a not-for-profit organization whose work spans 70 countries, including 45 where we have field conservation projects and another 25 where we contribute critical conservation funding. With the help of many conservation collaborators and generous donors, SDZG has been involved in reintroduction efforts for 46 species: 16 mammal species, 20 bird species, 9 species of reptiles and amphibians, and 1 invertebrate species.

SDZG also operates the San Diego Zoo and the San Diego Zoo Safari Park. With a combined 5 million visitors each year, the Zoo and the Safari Park provide guests with the opportunity to see thousands of plant and animal species in person and up close, including rare and endangered species that serve as ambassadors to inspire compassion for the plight of their wild counterparts.

San Diego Zoo Global has the largest zoological membership association in the world, with more than 430,000 members, including 100,000 child members of the San Diego Zoo Kids Club. The San Diego Zoo Global Wildlife Conservancy (endextinction.org) helps support our wildlife conservation efforts.

About the San Diego Zoo Safari Park

The Safari Park is an expansive wildlife sanctuary that is home to more than 3,000 animals representing approximately 300 species. Its renowned botanical collection represents 3,500 species and 1.75 million specimens. Nearly half of the Safari Park's 1,800 acres have been set aside as protected native species habitat. It is located 30 miles north of downtown San Diego in the San Pasqual Valley near Escondido, California.

About the San Diego Zoo

The 100-acre Zoo is home to more than 3,700 rare and endangered animals representing approximately 660 species and subspecies, and a prominent botanical collection with more than 700,000 exotic plants representing 25,000 species. It is located in Balboa Park just north of downtown San Diego.

About SDZG Conservation Efforts

SDZG's conservation efforts take many forms, involving a variety of departments within the organization. The key hub for this activity takes place at the San Diego Zoo Institute for Conservation Research (ICR), which is dedicated to saving plant and animal species worldwide by focusing its efforts in eight strategic areas:

- **Conservation Genetics:** *Sustaining and restoring genetic diversity through bioresource banking and research*
- **Reproductive Sciences:** *Applying innovative science and technology to enhance reproduction*
- **Population Sustainability**: *Integrating behavior and ecology to ensure population viability*
- **Disease Investigations**: *Removing disease as a roadblock to conservation*
- **Plant Conservation:** *Working across scientific disciplines to save rare plants*
- **Recovery Ecology:** *Adaptively managing and restoring species to the wild*
- **Community Engagement**: *Driving conservation action through science education and community collaborations*
- **Global Partnerships:** *Building collaborations with key partners to achieve shared conservation goals*

San Diego Zoo Global Online

At San Diego Zoo Global's online sites, guests can discover the many facets of the organization—from conservation work around the world to in-depth information about the animals and plants at the San Diego Zoo and the San Diego Zoo Safari Park.

Visit sandiegozooglobal.org to learn more about our parks and our fight to end extinction.

ABOUT THE AUTHOR

Beth Branning is the former chief strategy officer and director of Vision, Innovation, and Strategy (VIS) at San Diego Zoo Global (SDZG). The SDZG strategic planning process she developed received the 2013 Association for Strategic Planning (ASP) Goodman Award—the top international prize for strategic planning innovation and implementation.

For 15 years, Beth oversaw major planning efforts not only at SDZG but also with dozens of collaborators. Many of Beth's "clients" were endangered animals in desperate need of worldwide conservation strategies, including elephants, koalas, giant pandas, and desert tortoises. She helped multiorganizational groups—from the county of San Diego to the continent of Australia—collaborate to save wildlife. Beth also oversaw the strategic planning efforts for many nonprofit associations, including the American Alliance of Museums and the Association of Zoos and Aquariums.

Beth was first hired at SDZG as a writer in 1988, creating animal habitat graphics and marketing education programs. Eventually, she became head of strategic communications before she took the helm of the Vision, Innovation, and Strategy group. In 2017, Beth left SDZG to open Branning Strategies (branningstrategies.com), a strategic planning consultancy specializing in helping mission-driven organizations and associations to realize their potential.

Beth has a degree in journalism and is also certified as a Strategic Management Professional (SMP), the top certification offered by ASP. She has served on both the local and international boards of ASP and has received its distinguished Janice Laureen Award for outstanding leadership and guidance, as well as awards of excellence from the American Alliance of Museums, the Association of Zoos and Aquariums, the YWCA, and Athena San Diego.